Understanding Sustainable Architecture

Understanding Sustainable Architecture is a review of the assumptions, beliefs, goals and bodies of knowledge that underlie the endeavour to design (more) sustainable buildings and other built developments.

Much of the available advice and rhetoric about sustainable architecture begins from positions where important ethical, cultural and conceptual issues are simply assumed. If sustainable architecture is to be a truly meaningful pursuit then it must be grounded in a coherent theoretical framework. This book sets out to provide that framework. Through a series of self-reflective questions for designers, the authors argue the ultimate importance of reasoned argument in ecological, social and built contexts, including clarity in the problem framing and linking this framing to demonstrably effective actions. Sustainable architecture, then, is seen as a revised conceptualization of architecture in response to a myriad of contemporary concerns about the effects of human activity.

The aim of this book is to be transformative by promoting understanding and discussion of commonly ignored assumptions behind the search for a more environmentally sustainable approach to development. It is argued that design decisions must be based on both an ethical position and a coherent understanding of the objectives and systems involved. The actions of individual designers and appropriate broader policy settings both follow from this understanding.

Terry Williamson was educated in engineering and architecture in Australia and is Dean of the School of Architecture, Landscape Architecture and Urban Design at the University of Adelaide, Australia. **Antony Radford** was educated in architecture and planning in the United Kingdom and is Professor of Architecture at the University of Adelaide. **Helen Bennetts** was educated in architecture in Australia and, after researching how architects actually use information in seeking to produce environmentally responsible buildings, now concentrates on the family business of wine- and cheese-making. All three have taught, researched and published in areas of energy, environment and sustainability. This book draws particularly on their development and teaching of a new course called Issues in Urban and Landscape Sustainability.

Understanding Sustainable Architecture

**Terry Williamson,
Antony Radford
and Helen Bennetts**

London and New York

First published 2003 by Spon Press
11 New Fetter Lane, London EC4P 4EE

Simultaneously published in the USA and Canada by Spon Press
29 West 35th Street, New York, NY 10001

Spon Press is an imprint of the Taylor & Francis Group

© 2003 Terry Williamson, Antony Radford and Helen Bennetts

Typeset in 10/12pt Goudy by Graphicraft Limited, Hong Kong
Printed and bound in Great Britain by Biddles Ltd, Guildford and King's Lynn

British Library Cataloguing in Publication Data
A catalogue record for this book is available from the British Library

Library of Congress Cataloging in Publication Data
A catalog record for this book has been requested.

ISBN 0-415-28351-5 (hbk)
ISBN 0-415-28352-3 (pbk)

To our families – past, present and future generations

Contents

Preface

Towards the end of the twentieth century the word sustainable (and sustainability) entered into the consciousness of architects and became an essential concern in the discourse of architecture.

Our decision to write this book stemmed from two sources: research on how architects conceptualized sustainability in the design of houses, and the teaching of a course called Issues in Urban and Landscape Sustainability to students of architecture and landscape architecture. In both cases we found that although there is much written about the urgency of taking sustainability seriously, and much advice about building techniques to adopt, there was little which addressed the interrelated issues of the sociocultural, ethical, professional and technological complexities of 'sustainable architecture'. The following chapters record our understanding of these complexities. They are relatively self-contained, so that each chapter can be read alone.

Sustainable architecture is a revised conceptualization of architecture in response to a myriad of contemporary concerns about the effects of human activity. In this book we review the assumptions, beliefs, goals, processes and knowledge sources that underlie the endeavour to design buildings that address sustainability in environmental, sociocultural, and economic terms. Rather than providing 'how to' building advice or critically reviewing existing projects that claim to be examples of sustainable architecture, we aim to bring to the forefront some components of the milieu in which other books that do address these topics are positioned. We argue that the design of sustainable architecture must be grounded in an inclusive view of the scope of sustainability in each situation, and without such an approach attempts to use available published advice may in many ways be counterproductive.

In the core chapters of the book we address approaches to architectural sustainability. First, we consider the ways that sustainability is conceptualized in architecture. We then turn to questions about the ethical or moral bases of our decision-making and different perceptions of stakeholders, from anthropocentric 'human rights' or 'consequentialist' positions to a 'deep ecology' position in which humans have no more rights than other stakeholders in our planet. We suggest that sustainable architecture is most likely to result from the inclination of architects to perform *beautiful* acts. How this might be brought about leads to a discussion of the nature of architectural decision making, and the roles of guidelines and regulations as means-based and performance-based assertions of 'what should happen' in design. The reductionist approach inherent in most design guides, standards and regulations ignores the many contextual issues that surround sustainable designing. This is followed by an exploration of a way of thinking using a systems approach to building design combining both quantifiable and non-quantifiable factors. How the framing of objectives and advice is connected with larger political and economic concerns is illustrated in a discussion of the promotion of 'greener houses' in response to concerns about climate change, the dominant international environmental issue of our time. The final chapter of the book draws together this discussion, and addresses the question of how we might recognize design for truly sustainable architecture through a search for 'responsive cohesion'.

Our aim in this book is to be transformative by promoting understanding and discussion of commonly ignored assumptions behind the search for a more environmentally sustainable approach to development. We argue that design decisions must be based on both an ethical position and a coherent understanding of the objectives, processes and systems involved. The actions of individual designers and appropriate broader policy settings both follow from this understanding.

Acknowledgements

We thank many people: Peter Fawcett, Deborah White, Scott Drake, Mark Jackson and Garrett Cullity for reading and commenting on drafts of the book, Warwick Fox for his initial encouragement and guidance on responsive cohesion, Veronica Soebarto, Deborah White, Susan Pietsch, Dinah Ayers, Barry Rowney, Derrick Kendrick and Nguyen Viet Huong for their help and advice and our colleagues at the School of Architecture and Landscape Architecture at the University of Adelaide for their support. We particularly thank Susan Coldicutt for her wise counsel. We also acknowledge the Australian Research Council for funding a linked project on ethics, sustainability and houses. Finally we thank the students, present and past, who have motivated us to write this book.

Material from *The Hannover Principles* is reproduced by permission of William McDonough & Partners.

Material from *Our Common Future* by The World Commission on Environment and Development (1990) is reproduced by permission of Oxford University Press Australia © Oxford University Press, http://www.oup.com.au

Photographs are reproduced by permission of the photographers or other copyright holders: T. R. Hamzah & Yeang Sdn Bhd (photograph of the model of the EDITT Tower) Walter Dobkins (photographs of the Comesa Centre), Cradle Huts P/L (photograph of Kia Ora Hut), Richard Harris (photograph of Hollow Spruce), Barry Rowney (photograph of The Mosque at New Gourna), George Baird (photograph of Eastgate), Ian Lambot (photograph of Commerzbank).

Figure 2.1 is reproduced from K. Milton (ed.) *Environmentalism: the view from anthropology*, Routledge, London, 1993 with the permission of Taylor and Francis.

1.1 The fragile Earth: View over the moon from Apollo 8, 22 December 1968 (NASA).

1 Sustainability

At certain times in the practice of a discipline, concepts and strategies based on common themes or concerns can be seen to arise. The continuation, small shifts, fundamental transformations, or replacement of issues can be affected by institutional settings such as political events, changes in technologies, scientific discoveries, calamities (actual or imagined) or economic practices and processes. Viewed in this way, 'green', 'ecological', and 'environmental' are labels that embody the notion that the design of buildings should fundamentally take account of their relationship with and impact on the natural environment. The formation of these concepts can, more or less, be traced to the early 1970s. Emerging from the same period, labels such as 'low energy', 'solar' and 'passive' are used to denote approaches to designing concerned with the concept of reducing reliance on fossil fuels to operate a building. In general, the labels refer to a particular strategy employed to achieve the conceptual outcome, and the strategies that occur in a discourse must be understood as instances from a range of theoretical possibilities. The promotion of a restricted range of strategic options regulates the discourse and the ways of practising the discipline. An examination of sustainable design discourse and practice will reveal something of this regulation.[1] Overall, practitioners modify their concept of their discipline to embrace these new themes, concerns and ways of practice.[2]

Sustainable architecture, then, is a revised conceptualization of architecture in response to a myriad of contemporary concerns about the effects of human activity. The label 'sustainable' is used to differentiate this conceptualization from others that do not respond so clearly to these concerns.

Not long ago a major part of the image of good architecture was a building that was *suitable* for its environmental context – one that would adequately protect the inhabitants from the climate. More recently it is 'the environment' that has been seen as needing protection. The concept of good architecture has shifted to encompass the notion of a building that is *sensitive to* its environment – one that will adequately protect the environment from the potential pollution and degradation caused by human habitation. In many ways the built environment, the very means by which we attempt to create secure conditions, is itself seen as becoming (or having become) a source of danger and threat.

> At a certain point ... – very recently in historical terms – we started worrying less about what nature can do to us, and more about what we have done to nature. This marks the transition from the predominance of external risk to that of manufactured risk.
>
> (Giddens 1999a)

Manufactured risk is created by the impact we are having upon the world. It refers to risk situations which humans have never encountered, and which we therefore have no traditional experience in dealing with. They result directly from the applications of technology in response to the circumstances of increasing populations[3] and desired higher standards of living. Charles Jenks, best known as a critic writing on modern and postmodern architecture, states unequivocally:

> The problems of a modern technocratic civilization will always keep one step ahead of any amelioration because the reigning ideology of continual human growth – both numerical and economic – is unrealistic. It will continue to manufacture new problems, equivalents of the greenhouse effect and the hole in the ozone layer. No matter how many piecemeal solutions to these are instituted, the problems will go on multiplying because, for the first time in history, humanity rather than the Earth has become the dominant background. The players have become the stage.
>
> (Jenks 1993: 126–7)

Ultimately, then, manufactured risk is an issue that needs to be addressed. As Sylvan and Bennett observe,

> To be green in more than a token fashion is to have some commitment to containing or reducing the environmental impact of humans on the Earth or regions of it. ... [That] means commitment in the immediate future term to either:
>
> • human population reduction, or
> • less impacting lifestyles for many humans, or
> • improvements in technology to reduce overall impact.
>
> (Sylvan and Bennett 1994: 23)

This can be put succinctly in the form of the equation:

$$EI = P \times C \times T, \; or$$
Environmental Impact of a group = Population × Consumption × Technology

(Sylvan and Bennett 1994: 47)

The implication of this formula is that for the human race to continue indefinitely its environmental impact must be no more than the level that the world can sustain indefinitely, known as the 'carrying capacity' of the world's ecosystems.[4] However, this is not a static system; the environmental impact of humans changes over time (historically increasing, but neither the population, consumption nor the technology are constants and impacts can potentially decrease as well as increase). Perhaps, in the very long term, what happens does not really matter: humans are more likely to miss having a habitable world than what might be left of the world is likely to miss humans, and in a few more million years civilization might start all over again. The very idea that human action can destroy the Earth repeats in negative form the hubristic ambitions of those who seek complete human control of the world (Harvey 1998).[5]

> Perhaps the destiny of man is to have a short but fiery, exciting and extravagant life rather than a long, uneventful and vegetative existence. Let other species – the amoebas, for example – which have no spiritual ambitions inherit an Earth still bathed in plenty of sunshine.
>
> (Georgescu-Roegen 1993: 105)

But most of us would wish to avoid the more catastrophic prospects, at least during our own, our children's and our grandchildren's lifetimes. Buildings contribute directly and substantially to manufactured risk because of the amount of raw materials, energy and capital they devour and the pollutants that they emit, and architects therefore have a specific and significant professional role in reducing this risk.

ESD (?)

'Sustainable' is defined in dictionaries in terms of continuity and maintenance of resources, for example:

> sus.tain.able adj (ca. 1727) 1: capable of being sustained 2 a: of, relating to, or being a method of harvesting or using a resource so that the resource is not depleted or permanently damaged <~ techniques> <~ agriculture> b: of or relating to a lifestyle involving the use of sustainable methods <~ society> – sus.tain.abil.i.ty n
>
> (Merriam-Webster 1994)

This and similar definitions present sustainability from an essentially anthropocentric and instrumental position, concerned with how to maintain and even improve the quality of human life within the carrying capacity of supporting ecosystems. The acronym ESD is often adopted as fuzzy code expressing a concern for sustainability issues in the way that human beings impact on this carrying capacity in the future.[6] The meaning of E varies between *environmental*, *ecological* and even *economic*, while the D sometimes means *development* and sometimes *design*. While the S stands for *sustainable* (and *sustainability*), this term in recent usage has come to denote a broader perspective and a new way of looking at the world. It suggests, at least in western countries, a social and cultural shift, a different attitude to the world around us, and modified patterns and styles of living. It acknowledges that the problem is global in scale and related to the basic issue of population increase and the resulting effects of human existence on the Earth.

Some understandings of ESD include actions aimed at mitigating the perceived adverse effects on local communities of trends toward economic globalization and free trade, accepting an argument that sustainable design should necessarily express community differences. In these broad views the concept bundles together issues of long-term human sociocultural and economic health and vitality,[7] issues that may or may not be linked with a concern for the well being of 'the environment' 'for its own sake' rather than solely as a potential resource and necessary support for human beings. The sustainability of all three – environmental, sociocultural and economic systems – is sometimes called the 'triple bottom line' by which the viability and success of design and development should be assessed.

Taken literally, the term 'sustainable architecture' focuses on the sustainability of *architecture*, both as a discipline and a product of the discipline. It carries with it the imprecise and contested meanings embedded in ESD, and denotes broader ideas than any of the individual understandings of ESD, in particular, the notion of 'sustainable architecture' includes questions of a building's suitability for its sociocultural as well as environmental context. The associated question of 'What does sustainability mean for architecture?' forefronts architecture and looks for ways in which it must adapt. The question of 'What does architecture mean for sustainability?' forefronts sustainability and positions architecture as one amongst many contributing factors in achieving a meaningful human existence in a milieu of uncertainty.[8]

A global framework

In 1987, the World Commission on Environment and Development report *Our Common Future* (also known as the *Brundtland Report*) provided an early (and still much-used) authoritative definition of what constitutes sustainable development.[9] Thus, according to the *Brundtland Report*:

> Humanity has the ability to make development sustainable – to ensure that it meets the needs of the present without compromising the ability of future generations to meet their own needs . . . Sustainable development is not a fixed state of harmony, but rather a process of change in which the exploitation of resources, the direction of investments, the orientation of technological development, and institutional change are made consistent with future as well as present needs.
>
> (WCED 1990: 8)

This definition of sustainable development contains two crucial elements. First, it accepts the concept of 'needs', in particular those basic needs of the world's poor, such as food, clothing and shelter essential for human life, but also other 'needs' to allow a reasonably comfortable way of life. Second, it accepts the concept of 'making consistent' the resource demands of technology and social organizations with the environment's ability to meet present and future needs. This includes both local and global concerns and has a political dimension, embracing issues of resource control and the inequities that exist between developed and developing nations.[10] In this way it endorses the notion of sustainable development as improving (and not merely maintaining) the quality of life within the limits of the carrying capacity of supporting ecosystems.

The project to consider sustainability as an integral aspect of all development, following the lead of the Brundtland Commission, has been enshrined in international declarations, conventions and other plans for action. The Earth Summit held in June 1992 in Rio de Janeiro, Brazil, was a defining event in the sustainable development movement. Not only did it bring together an unprecedented number of countries, organizations and citizens from throughout the world, it represented the first time that developed and developing nations reached consensus on some difficult issues related to the environment and development. The summit adopted the *Rio Declaration on Environment and Development*, consisting of 27 principles that were put forward as a blueprint for achieving global sustainability.[11]

Principle 1 states that 'Human beings are at the centre of concerns for sustainable development. They are entitled to a healthy and productive life in harmony with nature.' Several important international agreements emerged from the Earth Summit: *Agenda 21* (United Nations 1992b), the *UN Framework Convention on Climate Change* (UNFCCC 1992a), the *UN Convention on Biological Diversity* (United Nations 1992c), and the *UN Convention to Combat Desertification in Those Countries Experiencing Serious Drought and/or Desertification* (United Nations 1992d).[12] While all four have some implications for sustainable architecture, two are more directly related.

Agenda 21 has the goal to 'halt and reverse the environmental damage to our planet and to promote environmentally sound and sustainable development in all countries on Earth'. Moving the discussion of sustainability from theory to a plan of action, *Agenda 21* sets out detailed proposals for communities throughout the world to adopt and implement specific measures centred on eight key objectives aimed at improving the social, economic and environmental quality of human settlements and the living and working environments of all people. These eight objectives are:

Providing adequate shelter,
Improving management of urban settlements,
Promoting sustainable land-use planning and management,
Providing environmentally sound infrastructure facilities,
Promoting energy-efficient technology, alternative and renewable energy sources and sustainable transport systems,
Enabling disaster-prone countries to plan for and recover from natural disasters,
Promoting sustainable construction industry activities, and finally
Human resource development.

The objective of the *Framework Convention on Climate Change* (UNFCCC 1992) is to slow down or halt suspected adverse changes of climate (in excess of anticipated natural climate variations) that may be attributable directly or indirectly to human activity. Since the operation of buildings makes a significant contribution to the production of carbon dioxide and other 'greenhouse gas' emissions that are held responsible for these changes of climate, this convention could have a far-reaching effect on the design of buildings. We shall discuss it, and policy and design changes that have followed for houses, in Chapter 6.

Within the discipline of architecture, a statement recognizing that building design professionals should frame their work in terms of sustainable design was made at the Union of International Architects' World Congress of Architects meeting in Chicago in June 1993. Embracing both environmental and social sustainability, the Congress asserted:

> We commit ourselves, as members of the world's architectural and building-design professions, individually and through our professional organizations, to:
> - Place environmental and social sustainability at the core of our practice and professional responsibilities;
> - Develop and continually improve practice, procedures, products, curricula, services and standards that will enable the implementation of sustainable design;
> - Educate our fellow professionals, the building industry, clients, students and the general public about the critical importance and substantial opportunities of sustainable design;
> - Establish policies, regulations, and practices in government and business that ensure sustainable design becomes normal practice;
> - Bring all existing and future elements of the built environment – in their design, production, use and eventual re-use – up to sustainable design standards.
>
> (UIA 1993)

The commitment was unequivocal but what does it mean – what follows from the commitment? We have already noted the imprecision associated with concepts of sustainable architecture and development, and 'sustainable design' is a label that has been assigned for many different reasons to many kinds of buildings, from a woven grass and thatch *bure* on a Pacific island to a high-tech office building in the United States. The former is reckoned to be a sustainable design because it is constructed entirely of biodegradable material and appropriates only a tiny amount of the world's resources for its construction, compared with a typical 'western' building. The office building may be considered an example of sustainable design if it requires significantly less energy for heating, cooling and lighting than is typical for its class. They both appear as manifestations of the values that have come to be associated with sustainability (von Bonsdorff 1993: 8). The implications for our conceptualization of architecture was apparent at the time. Susan Maxman, then President of the American Institute of

Architects (and with Olufemi Majekodunmi, then UIA President, named under the commitment) wrote that 'sustainable architecture isn't a prescription. It's an approach, an attitude. It shouldn't really even have a label. It should just be *architecture*' (Maxman 1993, quoted in Guy and Farmer 2001: 140).

A cultural/philosophical framework

In societies of European descent or influence three trademarks, dualism, reductionism and positivism, pervade modern living. They shape the way we think about problems, the way we make decisions and therefore the way we design buildings. Sustainability (and why we are discussing it as an issue) reflects the philosophical framework of these trademarks. The seventeenth-century thinker René Descartes is commonly credited with laying its foundations, and the effects have touched all aspects of human endeavour, from science to morality. Alberto Pérez-Gómez traces how this philosophical position influenced the way architecture was reconceptualized during the late eighteenth and nineteenth centuries in his book *Architecture and the Crisis of Modern Science* (Pérez-Gómez 1983).[13]

Probably the most significant of the trademarks, dualism expresses a distinction between body and mind, between matter and spirit, and between reason and emotion. By body/matter/reason is meant the extended or corporal world, everything beyond self-consciousness, a world in which all phenomena can be completely determined by mechanistic principles. This divide separates regular predictable and controllable events from those that are erratic, unpredictable and uncertain. Cartesian dualism effectively sets humans apart from nature, but also an individual self apart from 'the other' of everything outside the self. Conventionally, responsibility for 'the other' is dealt with by articulating codes of appropriate behaviour.

Science based disciplines operate by disconnecting 'anthropological reference from its description of the world' (Dripps 1999: 47). By definition, reason-determined solutions become the only true ones. The conventional application of economics to distribute resources, for example, 'treats the economy as a separate, mechanically reversible system, virtually independent of the ecosphere' (Rees 1999). Mind/spirit/emotion, on the other hand, together with all mental phenomena, is totally severed from sense experiences. Institutions as bureaucracies deal with people in terms of procedural rationality, where the emotions of an individual, as Bauman describes, that 'unruly voice of conscience that may prompt one to help the sufferer' (Bauman 1995: 260) is constrained and moral sentiments are exiled from the process.

The second trademark of modern living, reductionism, perceives all entities as consisting of simpler or more basic entities. From this derives a method of acquiring knowledge and thinking about issues that consists of breaking down a problem into simpler units, its component parts, in a process of atomization. We study and attempt to understand these simple units, and reassembling the parts in a 'logical' fashion shapes our understanding of the whole problem. The whole consists of the sum of the parts, no more and no less. Confidence in this process is evident in the trademark of positivism, belief in 'the infinite capacity of human reason to control, dominate, and put to work the forces of nature' so that eventually everything could be understood and managed (Pérez-Gómez 1983: 273).

The reconceptualization of architecture in response to Cartesian thinking retained a place for the 'mind/body/spirit' side of the duality. This led to the familiar distinction between the *science of architecture* and the *art of architecture*, as explained in a paper delivered to the Royal Institute of British Architects by Mark Hartland Thomas,

> Science communicates notions of quantities, verifiable by number, and intended to be the same for all men . . . Art, on the other hand, communicates notions of value, fantasy, never the same for any two recipients, no two responses being alike, although the relative importance of works of art does emerge from the sum total of many differing responses . . . It is commonplace that architecture partakes of science as well as of art.
>
> (Hartland Thomas 1948)[14]

An alternative approach conceived from a different philosophical perspective has emerged which offers both a critique of the conventional scientific paradigm and a different view for judging the appropriateness of actions. This approach derives from the notions of ecology as the science of the relationships between organisms and their environment; or of the relationship between a human group and its environment. In this view of the world, biotic organisms and non-biotic elements are integral parts of an ecosystem. In philosophical terms ecology goes beyond the limits of the analytical and empirical world of direct experience and enters the metaphysical realms, in which complete comprehension of the environment is essentially unknowable. We shall return to ecology and environmental ethics in Chapter 3. Ecology provides insights about how natural systems work, including systems subject to human interference. Indeed, natural systems ecology very often serves as a model that provides a scientific justification for sustainability. The absence of sustainability in natural systems is generally marked by two observations; resource demands in excess of absolute limits or variations imposed on the system whose rate of change is beyond the possibilities of adjustment. While perhaps providing a valuable insight into possible dangers it does carry a logical ambiguity. As Redclift (1994) points out, this discourse framed as an ecological view fails to connect into the image the issues of human choices and of human interventions.

While modernity continues as the dominant framework of architectural practice, (as manifest in its political context, legislation, regulations, design advice, and other practices), 'postmodern' theorists and critics point to the enormity of the predicaments we face and repudiate the modern ways of going about solving the problems.

> One of the practical dimensions of the crisis derives from the sheer magnitude of our powers. What we and other people do may have profound,

far-reaching and long-term consequences, which we can neither see directly nor predict with precision. Between the deeds and their outcomes there is a huge distance – both in time and in space – which we cannot fathom using our innate, ordinary powers of perception – and so we can hardly measure the quality of our actions by a full inventory of their effects. What we and others do has 'side-effects', 'unanticipated consequences', which may smother whatever good purposes are intentioned and bring about disasters and suffering neither we nor anybody else wished or contemplated.

(Bauman 1993: 17–18)

Science has become one of the most influential ways of understanding the world, and this institutionalized confidence and scientific methodology has led to new technologies that have contributed to material well-being and health for many people. It has, though, also brought with it the invention of hideous weapons of destruction and the extravagant use of limited resources. Considering the world as something to be exploited and manipulated for human purposes has resulted in the destruction and pollution of much of the natural environment and the extinction of whole species. Michael Redclift illustrates the way that sustainability relates to both modernist and postmodern views:

The idea of sustainability is derived from science, but at the same time highlights the limitations of science. It is used to carry moral, human, imperatives, but at the same time acquires legitimacy from identifying biospheric 'imperatives' beyond human sciences. Married to the idea of development, sustainability represents the high-water mark of Modernist tradition. At the same time, emphasis on cultural diversity, which some writers view as the underpinning of sustainability, is a clear expression of Postmodernism.

(Redclift 1994: 17)

The manageable (but fragile) Earth

Maarten Hajer links the way that environmental issues are now framed and understood to the photographs of planet Earth taken from outer space during the Apollo space missions. The earliest of these photographs, taken during the Apollo 8 mission of 1968, records the first time that humans had travelled far enough from Earth to obtain an image that showed the whole planet. Hajer sees this image as marking a 'fundamental shift in thinking about the relationship between man and nature' (Hajer 1995: 8) with conflicting impressions of a world that is both bounded and manageable (and therefore amenable to the tools of the scientific tradition) and small and vulnerable (and therefore fragile and easily damaged by human carelessness).[15] Andrew Ross, in his book *The Chicago Gangster Theory of Life*, captures this impression of fragility and callous human carelessness:

The clichés of the standard environmental image are well known to us all: on the one hand, belching smokestacks, seabirds mired in petrochemical sludge, fish floating belly-up, traffic jams in Los Angeles and Mexico City, and clearcut forests; on the other hand, the redeeming repertoire of pastoral imagery, pristine, green and unspoiled by human habitation, crowned by the ultimate global spectacle, the fragile, vulnerable ball of spaceship Earth.

(Ross 1994: 171)

Two responses to this new popular concern about the degrading environment are, continuing Ross's appeal to stereotypes, first a call to 'repent for tomorrow is the end' by the 'prophets of doom', and second claims that 'we have the answer' from the 'snake-oil peddlers'. The first manifests itself in unsubstantiated and exaggerated claims about the future implications of possible environmental impacts, and the second in unsubstantiated and exaggerated claims about the future benefits of products or processes. The 'prophets of doom' simplify the complex and uncertain research into the actual relationships between climate and human impact into the presentation of alarming scenarios as scientifically-authenticated certainties. This is dangerous because it leads to a misallocation of effort and resources and masks valid concerns. The 'snake oil peddlers' present products of all kinds, including buildings, as offering qualities of sustainability and environmental friendliness. 'Greenness, suddenly, is marketable' (Fisher 1994: 33). This phenomenon of eco-labelling has been given the title 'greenwash' (Greer and Bruno 1996). Garden furniture made in Vietnam and using timber taken from virgin forests in Cambodia, Laos and Burma has been branded Ecoline with a label that reads: 'This article is an environmental-friendly product. For every fallen tree a new one is planted so no tropical rainforest need be destroyed' (Tickell 1999). The organization Friends of the Earth revealed that the logging of this timber was often highly destructive, often illegal and often took place in national parks and reserves intended to protect endangered wildlife. In France, a large supermarket chain sold a similar range, but in this case the origin was not identified. On each table and chair was simply a tag bearing a vague Asian graphic and a statement that

> *Le maranti dint sont fabriqué vos meuble de jardin provient de foréts gérées dans le but de mantenir un parfait equilibre écologique.* (The merranti that is used to make this garden furniture comes from forests managed with the aim of maintaining a perfect ecological equilibrium.)

If, as advertising people say, marketing is mainly about selling concepts and lifestyles that just happen to have products attached, then the fact that such statements exist is a testament to the degree the sustainability issue has penetrated the public consciousness in these countries. Sometimes these statements are misrepresentations made in ignorance rather than with the intention to mislead or deceive. Often, however, a fraudulent intention seems clear – there are lies, damned lies and claims for sustainability.

Without some form of authoritative certification such statements are worthless. For timber, such an authoritative certification system does exist. The Forest Stewardship Council (FSC) was established in 1993 as a worldwide standard-setter for socially and environmentally beneficial forestry. FSC accredits independent certifiers to audit forestry practices against its standards. Products made of timber from certified forests may carry the FSC logo. It is the only eco-label for timber approved by the major environmental groups. But even this guide can have pitfalls, as an Australian architect discovered. She specified 'that only certified plantation grown, Australian eucalypt timber' should be used for parquetry flooring of a dwelling. The 'specified' timber arrived on site in packages labelled *Fabricado em Portugal*. It was unclear whether the timber had been grown in Portugal or logs had been transported there for manufacture into the flooring product.

There is much 'doom and greenwash' in the discourse of architecture. The doom is apparent in some of the rhetoric of government and other agencies, used as a means to attract attention following the principle that the ends justify the means. The greenwash is manifest in some of the claims made for the plethora of building materials, features and gadgets that by their presence alone are held to authenticate a green building. Sometimes these are rustic materials (mud brick, straw bales, rammed earth). Sometimes they are high-tech gadgets (solar panels, sun scoops and geothermal heating systems). The important point is that while biodegradable materials and technical devices can make effective contributions, and symbolic elements can be important in their own right (we discuss this later), the use of such materials and devices is not *alone* a sufficient indicator of an environmentally friendly building. There must be demonstrable benefits in the particular case. Many ecogadgets do not really justify in use the environmental and financial cost of their production, and many buildings do not operate (or are operated by their occupants) as imagined. Drawing arrows on building cross sections, for example, does not mean that airflow will cooperatively follow the indicated path. This point was nicely made in a paper entitled 'Air is stupid (It can't follow the arrows)' (Were 1989).[16] Showing a photograph of an ancient middle-eastern windcatcher on a new design proposal for another place does not mean that the careful and effective cooling effect achieved after hundreds of years of development for the original local climate will be transferred to the new building. So far there has been remarkably little systematic post-construction measurement and evaluation of buildings for which claims of 'sustainable architecture' are made.

We can parallel the notion of 'ecogadgets' by coining the term 'cultureclamps', those devices which relate to sustainability in cultural rather than physical environment terms. This refers to the assumption that a global building designed elsewhere can be clamped limpet-like to a local culture by using the 'right' materials, features and gadgets appropriated from the vernacular. Examples are corrugated iron denoting Australianness, grass roofs in South Pacific resort hotels, and half-timbered walls in English country villages. There is nothing intrinsically wrong or right about such styles and features, and their use may well be a careful contextual approach rather than a part of what we might call 'culturewash'. In the final chapter of this book we shall look to reasoned argument to distinguish between expressions of environmental and cultural sensitivity on the one hand, and of greenwash and culturewash on the other hand.

Towards a basis for action

Given this situation, how should architects and other designers respond? We have to *act*; to make decisions in our day-to-day practices as designers. There are checklists of recommended design actions in many books and web sites, and we add yet another in the Appendix of this book, which we shall introduce in Chapter 4. For each checklist the emphasis that is given to a recommendation depends partly on the moral position implicitly taken by the author. Some green architects such as William McDonough have set down principles upon which they believe sustainable design should be based. The following nine points, known as the Hannover Principles, were developed when McDonough was commissioned by the city of Hannover, Germany, to develop guidelines of design for sustainability for the Expo 2000 World's Fair.

1   Insist on rights of humanity and nature to coexist in a healthy, supportive, diverse and sustainable condition.

2   Recognize interdependence. The elements of human design interact with and depend upon the natural world, with broad and diverse implications at every scale. Expand design considerations to recognizing even distant effects.

3   Respect relationships between spirit and matter. Consider all aspects of human settlement including community, dwelling, industry, and trade in terms of existing and evolving connections between spiritual and material consciousness.

4   Accept responsibility for consequences of design decisions upon human well-being, the viability of natural systems, and their rights to coexist.

5   Create safe objects of long-term value. Do not burden future generations with requirements for maintenance or vigilant administration of potential danger due to careless creation of products, processes, or standards.

6   Eliminate the concept of waste. Evaluate and optimize the full life cycle of products and processes, to approach the state of natural systems, in which there is no waste.

7   Rely on natural energy flows. Human designs should, like the living world, derive their creative forces from perpetual solar income. Incorporate this energy efficiently and safely for responsible use.

8   Understand the limitation of design. No human creation lasts forever and design does not solve all problems. Those who create and plan should practice humility in the face of nature. Treat nature as a model and a mentor, not an inconvenience to be evaded or controlled.

9   Seek constant improvement by the sharing of knowledge. Encourage direct and open communication between colleagues, patrons, manufacturers, and users to link long term sustainable considerations with ethical responsibility, and re-establish the integral relationship between natural processes and human activity.

(McDonough, William and Partners 1992: 5)

These recommendations are welcome and generally valid. They do, though, mix references to stakeholders (humanity and nature, principle 1), objectives ('do not burden future generations with requirements for maintenance', principle 5), means to achieve objectives ('incorporate [solar] energy efficiently and safely for responsible use', principle 7), and design approaches ('encourage direct and open communication between colleagues, patrons, manufacturers, and users', principle 9).[17] At best, checklists show a range of possibilities; at worse they risk giving a confusing indication of how to proceed in design. They do not necessarily help people design (though that is usually their intent), and may actually mislead because they cannot cope with the complexities and uniqueness of a particular design situation. In this sense they can be 'unecological', given that the concept of ecology has taught us to take account of complexity, interconnectedness and uniqueness.

This, then, is the context in which we write this book. Our topic is the way in which sustainable architecture is and should be conceptualized, and the beliefs, goals, processes and advice that underlie its promotion. Our aim is to inform this conceptualization by promoting discussion and understanding of commonly ignored assumptions behind the search for a more sustainable architecture, arguing that design decisions must be based on a coherent understanding of ethical stances and the objectives and systems involved. Individual actions and appropriate broader policies both follow from this understanding. Rather than providing 'how to' advice or critically reviewing existing projects that claim to be examples of sustainable architecture, we shall place in the forefront the milieu in which other books that do address these topics are positioned and read. We address our book primarily to other architects and future architects.[18]

In approaching our aim some of the questions that arise are:

- How is 'architectural sustainability' conceptualized?
- Does ethics offer a basis for action?
- Who or what are the stakeholders?
- How far can indicators of sustainability be quantified and understood in terms of the behaviour of systems?
- How do we deal with non-commensurable objectives and advice?
- How can we make and recognize sustainable architecture?

In dealing with these questions we argue that the notion of 'sustainable architecture' as a product, as attributes of buildings, is not only problematic but often counterproductive as it can lead to simplification and the undervaluing of local cultural and physical contexts. Instead, we advocate a way of thinking based on performing *beautiful acts* that arise out of *credible reasoned argument*, with a recognition of the way our values and our knowledge inform this process. We argue that:

- 'Sustainable architecture' is a cultural construction in that it is a label for a revised conceptualization of architecture;
- Within this revised conceptualization, by designing (more) 'sustainable architecture' we perform a 'beautiful act';
- A 'sustainable design' is a creative adaptation to ecological, sociocultural and built contexts (in that order of priority), supported by credible cohesive arguments.

In the following chapters we shall examine some of the key approaches that are promoted in the discourse of sustainability in architecture and building. We shall compare competing images of architectural sustainability that are apparent in the contemporary discourse of architecture. We shall consider ethical frameworks for practice. We shall locate regulations and design guides as means-based or performance-based statements about 'what should happen' in design. We shall explore the possibilities of systems theory with its assumption of the possibility of quantification and auditing of the life cycle impacts of the production, life, demolition and recycling of buildings. We shall examine the way that proposed responses to environmental impacts of buildings are connected with larger political and economic concerns. Finally we shall summarize individual and policy directions that might follow from the arguments set out in this exposition.

Notes

1 Foucault sees such strategies as 'systematically different ways of treating objects of discourse . . . of manipulating concepts (of giving them rules for their use, inserting them into regional coherences, and thus constituting conceptual architectures)' (Foucault 1972: 70). An analysis of competing conceptions of ecological place-making in the products and literature of architecture is made by Simon Guy and Graham Farmer (2000 and 2001). We shall explore this theme in Chapter 2.
2 See Donald Schön (1982: 103):

> At any given time in the life of a profession, certain ways of framing problems and roles come into good currency. . . . Their frames determine their strategies of attention and thereby set the directions in which they will try to change the situation, the values which will shape their practice. . . . When a practitioner becomes aware of his frames, he also becomes aware of the possibility of alternative ways of framing the realities of his practice. He takes note of the values and norms to which he has given priority, and those he has given less importance, or left out of account altogether. Frame awareness tends to entrain awareness of dilemmas.

3 The world population at the start of the twenty-first century was around six billion. Population projections are inherently unreliable. A 2001 study by the International Institute for Applied Systems Analysis in Laxenberg, Austria reported in *Nature*,

August 2001, suggested a peak of nine billion by 2070 with a population in decline by the end of this century.

4 When applied to sustainability, Seidl and Tisdell (1999) suggest that 'carrying capacity', rather than being a universal constraint, is a normative political concept to be understood only in terms of complex ecological dynamics together with the human social and institutional settings. The report of the Club of Rome *Limits to Growth* (Meadows 1972) focused awareness on the relationships between population, economic growth and environmental degradation. 'If the present growth trends in world population, industrialization, pollution, food production, and resource depletion continue unchanged, the limits to growth on this planet will be reached sometime within the next one hundred years' (Meadows 1972: 23). If we regard a decline in human population as desirable (by no means a universally accepted position), then we might use our professional skills to help raise living standards in the Third World with an expectation that lower birth rates will follow. This may be a desirable end, but Peter Fawcett responds:

> It is often argued that, because population growth is greatest in the underdeveloped countries, and because birth rates are lowered by affluence, world population increase can be limited by economic growth in poorer countries towards Western standards. There are two fallacies in this argument. Firstly, population continues to grow in even the richest countries; and secondly, the trade-off of consumption increase against reduction in population increase will take the ecosystem beyond limits. The total impact . . . will rise unless technology is cleaned up, affluence is restrained and population is limited.
>
> (Fawcett 1998: 64)

5 David Harvey continues:

> It is crucial to understand that it is materially impossible for us to destroy the planet Earth, that the worst we can do is to engage in material transformations of our environment so as to make life less rather than more comfortable for our own species, while recognizing that what we do also does have ramifications (both positive and negative) for other living species.
>
> (Harvey 1998: 328)

6 In Australia the description 'ecologically sustainable development' was coined in 1989 while developing policy directions to help resolve the socially divisive politics between competing environmental and developmental interests. This process started with an initiative led by the then Prime Minister Bob Hawke, who in 1989 released a Statement on the Environment, entitled *Our Country, Our Future*, and culminated in the release in 1992 of a *National Strategy for Ecologically Sustainable Development* (The ESD Strategy) that set out four main tenets:

- The Precautionary Principle – that measures to prevent environmental degradation should not be postponed due to lack of full scientific certainty.
- Intergenerational equity – that resources are left in trust for the benefit of future generations.
- Conservation of biological diversity – that measures should be undertaken to preserve genetic, species and ecosystem diversity and integrity.
- Environmental economic valuation, implying that the true cost of environmental impacts should be factored into the market economy.

The strategy has been endorsed in national and local government, for example, the Environmental Management policy of Central Sydney Development Control Plan

(CSDCP 1996) requires that 'principles of ecologically sustainable development (ESD) are integrated into the design and construction of development'. Similar positions have been taken in other countries.

7   While the growing use of the term [sustainable development] has led to a loss of clarity which needs to be addressed, what is important for us about sustainable development is its recognition of interconnections between a number of crucial areas. These are: environmental degradation; inequality; the future stability of society and the environment; and lastly, participation in and control of the decisions which affect these areas.

(Smith, Whitelegg and Williams 1998: 10)

8   People may ask – 'what does sustainability mean for architecture?' but perhaps the proper question is – 'what does architecture mean for sustainability?' The former question suggests a 'weak' approach to sustainability, i.e. an implicit assumption that sustainability has implications (possibly serious) for our present ways of procuring the built environment but those ways are basically appropriate. The latter question recognizes sustainability as the overarching concern, in terms of which all social disciplines and conduct must be reinterpreted and reformulated.

(Fawcett 1998: 68)

9 In the words of the Commission Chair, Gro Harlem Brundtland, then Prime Minister of Norway:

The environment does not exist as a sphere separate from human actions, ambitions, and needs, and attempts to defend it in isolation from human concerns have given the very word 'environment' a connotation of naivety in some political circles. The word 'development' has also been narrowed by some into a very limited focus, along the lines of 'what poor nations should do to become richer', and thus again is automatically dismissed by many in the international arena as being a concern of specialists, of those involved in questions of 'development assistance'. . . . But the 'environment' is where we all live; and 'development' is what we all do in attempting to improve our lot within that abode. The two are inseparable. Further, development issues must be seen as crucial by the political leaders who feel that their countries have reached a plateau towards which other nations must strive. Many of the development paths of the industrialized nations are clearly unsustainable. And the development decisions of these countries, because of their great economic and political power, will have a profound effect upon the ability of all peoples to sustain human progress for generations to come. . . . Many critical survival issues are related to uneven development, poverty, and population growth. They all place unprecedented pressures on the planet's lands, waters, forests, and other natural resources, not least in the developing countries. The downward spiral of poverty and environmental degradation is a waste of opportunities and of resources. In particular, it is a waste of human resources. These links between poverty, inequality, and environmental degradation formed a major theme in our analysis and recommendations. What is needed now is a new era of economic growth – growth that is forceful and at the same time socially and environmentally sustainable.

(WCED 1990: xv–xvi)

The World Commission for Economic Development was the first global effort to address the issue of sustainable development. It was also the first international policy advice document that acknowledged and focused on the interrelations between the economy and environmental well-being.

10 Some in fact have suggested that issues that are presented as serious threats to sustainability, such as resource depletion and global warming, are entirely political phenomena, examples of what the American journalist and satirist Henry Louis Mencken described thus: 'The whole aim of practical politics is to keep the populace alarmed – and hence clamorous to be led to safety – by menacing it with an endless series of hobgoblins, all of them imaginary' (Reproduced from Favourite Quotes: H.L. Mencken, Online. Available HTTP: http://www.geocities.com/Athens/Delphi/7248/mencken.html (January 2002).

11 For the full text of the Rio Declaration on Environment and Development; see Online. Available HTTP: http://www.unep.org/unep/rio.html (January, 2002).

12 These are published together as the 'Rio Cluster' of UN Proceedings, Online. Available HTTP: http://www.igc.org/habitat/un-proc/index.html (March 2002).

13 Pérez-Gómez concentrates on writing and work in France which led up to and followed Nicolas-Louis Durand's two famous theoretical books: the *Recueil et Paralléle des Edifices de Tout Genre, Anciens et Modernes* (1801), a large collection of drawings of building examples; and the *Précis des Leçons d'Architecture* (1802), which presented the content of his courses at the *École Polytechnique*.

14 This distinction implies that the 'science' and 'art' could be pursued separately, and even today the staffing and presentation of the discipline in schools of architecture commonly articulates and reinforces this perception.

15 Ingold (1993) maintains that the world view that locates the viewer outside the world with the Earth seen as a globe is associated with the triumph of modern science and technology. It carries implications that the Earth is something that can be conceived of as a whole and known objectively.

16   The trouble is, of course, that the air passing through the building has not seen the drawing. Even if it had, it would not be able to follow (understand) the arrows and, even if it could, it would not be able to follow the arrows (path) because air is stupid.

(Were 1989)

17 In Chapter 4 we shall locate these in a 'decision theory' model of the relations between decisions, means, objectives and other components of a purposeful design process.

18 We, as authors, are not viewing the world dispassionately from outside, observing what is happening and making an independent and objective record. We are down here in the world, carrying our own cultural baggage and taking part in the discourse and practice of architecture. As authors, our own collective background is western-educated (Australia and England) in architecture, engineering and planning, with a research and practice record that has been dominated by modernism.

2 Images

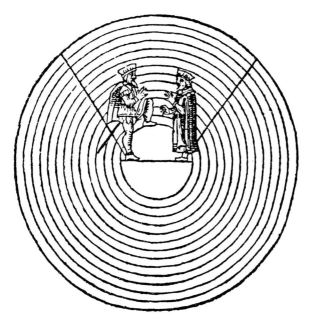

2.1 The fourteen spheres of the world, from Scala Naturale 1564 by Giovanni Camillo
Maffei (Ingold 1993: 33).

Fields of significance

We noted in Chapter 1 that in modern Western societies discussions of
sustainability are almost invariably associated with a particular way of looking
at the 'environment' that is scientific in nature and global in scope. Environmental problems such as climate change, acid rain and the depletion of the
ozone layer are essentially 'modern' in that they are global concerns, identified
using scientific methods, and involve international cooperation and national
institutions in their solution. The very expression 'the global environment'

makes this scope explicit, but even when we leave out the term 'global' the way that environmental issues are discussed often implies that there is just one big environment that we can somehow stand outside and comprehend (Cooper 1992: 167). But we can also think of environmental issues in terms of 'the environment' as it affects us in our day-to-day lives, as in 'the home environment' or 'the work environment'. This is not just a narrower or more selected version of the global view. It is a quite different perspective based on *knowing from within* that environment, and can never be fully appreciated from the 'outside'. It has connections to ancient views about the relationship of the individual to the world that were conceptualized as a person at the centre of a series of spheres (see Figure 2.1). The individual's view of the world grew from his or her local knowledge and personal and immediate experience and was drawn ever deeper into the world.

The medieval Judeo-Christian view of the universe placed the static, spherical earth at its centre with the stars attached to a surrounding, rotating sphere that marked the edge of the universe. The cosmology was rich in sign and symbol, with one of the central motifs being that nature was a book through which God's word could be read. David Cooper suggests that these notions of the environment were 'local' not so much in terms of geographical proximity or causal impact, but rather because one's environment was where one was 'at home', knew one's way around, and knew what things meant and stood for. People generally had a sense of belonging and identity that was intimately related to places and things (Cooper 1992).[1] Cooper talks of the environment as a 'field of significance' in which features and patterns of behaviour have acquired significance because of their importance in everyday practices. For example, a tree may have significance because it marks the halfway point of the walk home, because one's grandfather planted it or because it produces a wonderful crop of early apricots. These environments are known experientially through the senses as well as understood intellectually. Being at the centre of things, it is difficult for an individual to define the extent of his or her environment, but its sustainability for the individual entails the continuation of the myriad significances for that individual. Cooper refers to Heidegger's description of the 'referential totality' of a farm where items such as a cow's udder and a milk pail 'take on significance only as parts of a whole' (Cooper 1992: 170). According to Heidegger the sense of 'dwelling', of deep connection to land and place, is central to living and well-being. He asks us to

> Think for a while of a farmhouse in the Black Forest, which was built some two hundred years ago by the dwelling of peasants. Here the self-sufficiency of the power to let earth and heaven, divinities and mortals enter *in simple oneness* into things, ordered the house.
>
> (Heidegger 1971: 160)

The Black Forest farmhouse and other indigenous regional architectures of the kind that Rudofsky captured in his 1964 exhibition and book *Architecture Without*

Architects[2] (Rudofsky 1964) originate through practical and pragmatic choices based on the availability of local materials and the nature of local climate. They acquire a role in local culture and identity by 'being there' as a part of local life, a basis for sharing and participation. Over time, the technical and tectonic potential of modes of construction were developed to enrich the symbolic qualities of buildings, particularly those with religious or other particular cultural significance such a Norwegian stave church, a Greek temple or a Sarawak long-house.

In these terms, sustainability implies the potential to continue dwelling indefinitely, maintaining this connection to land and place. The land is instrumentally valuable in making cultivation possible, but equally important is its emotional role in a meaningful life. Further, family and society become intertwined with land and place, so that people belong in specific places in specific kinds of environments. To some peoples (including Australian Aborigines and Canadian Inui), elements of the landscape themselves have great spiritual significance. People 'belong' to a particular land area even if living elsewhere, and that area contains 'sacred sites' that only initiated members of the community know about and which must not be disturbed. Sustainability is then the protection and maintenance of existing land with all of its meanings.[3] But if we live in a (mythical) stable and an undisturbed local society, sustainability is not an issue. Our neighbours share our own cultural horizons, change is slow, and building form, culture and environmental change move in step. They have a similar field of significance and similar images of the world to our own.

By 'images' in this book we mean both the visual image (the most common meaning of the word) and what occurs '*behind* the eye', the way we represent ideas to ourselves and to others and the impressions we have of other people, products and things. As Kenneth Boulding (1961) described the concept in the early 1960s, images in this sense are about memory and imagination, connections to the past and to the future.[4] They can be likened to subjective knowledge, or what one believes to be true, and encapsulate not only verifiable 'facts' but values and emotions. Images are built up from a wide range of sources including personal experience, education, the media and our relationships with others. This is most familiar to architects through the writing of Kevin Lynch about the images that people have of cities and how these help in way-finding and 'reading' a city. He talks of the environmental image as:

> The generalized mental picture of the exterior physical world that is held by an individual. The image is both the product of immediate sensation and of the memory of past experience, and it is used to interpret information and to guide action.
>
> (Lynch 1960: 4)

Lynch maintains that the mental images that people have of a place: 'are organized structures of recognition and relationship. They are also suffused with meaning, feeling, and value, and these meanings are more complex and subtle than are the dry bones of structure' (Lynch 1976: 112–13).

The very nature of images means that they cannot be defined rigidly. Rather, these descriptions indicate the scope and possibilities of images: their multi-faceted nature, the importance of the pictorial or visual element, the ability to incorporate values, meaning, beliefs, and emotions, and the strong connection with memory.

An appreciation of the importance of one's own environments may provide the basis for confronting modern environmental problems. Cooper argues:

> The concerns . . . will begin 'at home', with *their* environments, the networks of meanings with which *they* are daily engaged. And these concerns will be directed at whatever threatens to separate them from their environment, to make their milieu alien. They will be directed, say, at the proposed erection of a factory farm, the squawking and stench from which expel the familiar sounds and smells of their surroundings; or at the planned construction of a motorway which will render impossible the old intimacy between neighbours on opposite sides of the valley.
>
> (Cooper 1992: 170)

Awareness of other cultures and other people's fields of significance changes assumptions from *the way things are* to a very different acknowledgment of *the way things are now for me*. Cooper continues:

> But these concerns will not remain purely 'local'. While my environmental concerns begin with *my* environment, I recognize that other people (and animals, too) have, or should have, their environments. If I appreciate the importance for my life of a place I know my way about I must appreciate the importance this has for others as well, and I will want to defend their efforts to preserve such places.
>
> (Cooper 1992: 170)

World citizens and pluralism

The latter part of the twentieth century and the opening of our current century have been marked by globalization and global issues that are not readily addressed within the boundaries of the nation state. We have transnational corporations that cross boundaries and whose immense resources are necessary to respond to major resource projects. We have political and economic migration where people cross political boundaries in order to seek a better life for themselves and their children. We have global issues such as terrorism and climate change that cannot be addressed within individual nations. We have international news media, increasingly integrated multinational political and economic groupings and agencies such as the European Economic Community, the World Bank and the International Monetary Fund. We have international law and multinational agreements such as the General Agreement on Tariffs and Trade.

Few people experience a single, geographic, place-based field of significance in our current century.[5] Conventionally the discussion of culture has concentrated on national and regional groups and their horizons, but national and regional boundaries are no longer effective markers in a world made smaller by communications and migration. There are cultural groups of international financiers and politicians as well as local fishermen. Further, cultures have 'ill-defined edges', so that people do not always clearly belong, or not belong, to a particular culture. Individuals are typically members of several overlaid cultural groups, with professional, religious, racial, national and other affiliations. The contemporary citizen is culturally hyphenated: a green-architect-Italian-American-something else; and along with the notion of the 'culturally hyphenated' is the notion of multiple fields of significance.

This view acknowledges that there are many environments that are defined in relation to their significance to 'that which is environed': an individual may recognize several environments and different individuals will recognize different environments. For many people, their images associated with the term 'environment' encompass both global and individual views. They shift focus easily between the global view and the individual field of significance views depending on the context in which environmental considerations arise.

We have, then, a world in which there is a tension between the international 'world citizen' horizon and the traditional 'race and place' horizon, and tensions between such concepts as universal human rights and local religious and cultural rights. Francis Fukuyama, who famously suggested that we had reached the end of history because the universal appeal of liberal democracy and free markets marked the end of the progress of humans towards modernity (Fukuyama 1992), argues that this process indeed threatens the traditional existence of some societies. For the modernist world citizen, place is just another commodity. Whether to live on a Greek island, in a Scandinavian forest, or in an American city is a choice made on the way that these places enable different lifestyles (including economic opportunities and climate), not on a sense of belonging and identity in the Heideggarian sense. Local culture – and local modes of building and architectural style – are facets of the commodity of place. Like the land itself, they may be embraced and valued, but they never carry the same deep meaning for the global itinerant dweller as they do for the native. Spector makes this point in *The Ethical Architect*:

> Modernists unapologetically maintain that globalization, scientific rationality, and technology are the most important elements of any context in this day and age; climate, history, and topography must be dealt with, of course, but they are easily dispatched. This attitude, simply put, is what it means to be modern.
>
> (Spector 2001: 162)

To the modernist world citizen, then, sustainability is construed primarily as the economic and environmental sustainability of our planet *as a whole*, with the continuation of this 'progress' towards modernity and increased personal freedom. It is seen predominantly in terms of global issues: protection of climate, resource conservation, biodiversity and cultural diversity, and economic stability as desirable features of the planet as a whole. When the regional and particular culture, economy, climate or ecosystem is addressed, this is done as instances of multiple particulars and with a constant awareness of the 'others'. It cannot be otherwise. Indeed, this book is a typical enterprise of the modernist world citizen; it tries to address global issues from our own cultural positions, with a desire to be instrumental (at least in a small way) on a global scale, and does so through the global publishing industry.

The international culture of architecture

Both the discourse and practice of architecture are increasingly dominated by global itinerants. Students of architecture are educated in architecture schools where staff may come from many countries, are taught with reference to globally-published reference books, are referred to the same iconic and emblematic buildings, and take part in international student competitions. When seeking information and knowledge they are likely to try an internet search engine before the shelves of their own library; indeed, if looking for a book they may well try Amazon.com before the library catalogue. The products of architecture are made known through international journals. The international strength of the disciplinary culture of architecture, with a small number of 'superstar' architects working concurrently in different parts of the world, dominates local contexts. The international offices share expertise across national boundaries, and their buildings are subject to internationally-agreed codes and standards. The growth of the multinational architectural firm leads to a divorce between the places where architectural design takes place (in 'design-oriented' ateliers), where documentation is carried out, where skilled people command lower salaries, and where the building is to be constructed. The 'meanings' associated with the building are those of global organizations and world citizens. Where the importance of local 'meaning' is recognized, it tends to be treated as something that can be 'given' to a building by designers for whom it is not meaningful, as just another 'function' of architecture.[6]

Modernism has accepted and celebrated internationalism with its manifest benefits, but at the same time as the practice and production of architecture is becoming more global and undifferentiated, the theory and discourse of the discipline is paying increasing attention to regional and national differences. Yet this recognition is not equivalent to operating from *inside* a culture. Theories of vernacularism, regionalism, critical regionalism, cross-cultural difference and heritage conservation are essentially perspectives on what happens locally seen from the position of the global citizen.

Simon Guy and Graham Farmer (2000, 2001) show through a social constructivist analysis how competing conceptions of ecological place-making in contemporary products and literature of architecture tend to create 'centres of gravity' and 'structuring' within the wider architectural discourse. This structuring 'is not created in abstraction as a recognition of purely contemporary concerns for environmental issues, it is also a reflection of a long and complex intermingling of architectural history' (Guy and Farmer 2000: 141). The rhetoric and terminology change to follow each paradigm. They cite eco-technic, eco-centric, eco-aesthetic, eco-cultural, eco-medical and eco-central logics, where a 'logic' is 'a specific ensemble of ideas, concepts and categorizations that are produced, reproduced and transformed in a particular set of practices through which meaning is given to social and physical realities' (Hajer 1995: 44). This has similarities to Boulding's 'image', but emphasizes the cultural analysis of a phenomenal structure rather than the mental concept. A particular building project might be described in a journal using one or several (but rarely many) of these structures. Each of them has dominant concerns, dominant local or global horizons, and appears to privilege particular kinds of building character. Some may be shared with other professions; the 'eco-social' logic, for example, is shared with planners and the 'eco-technic' is the one most closely aligned with the scientific paradigm of engineering.

Here we shall present just three contrasting images of architectural sustainability which we shall call, as shorthand for the complex association of ideas that they embody, the natural image, the cultural image, and the technical image (Table 2.1). The three images are caricatures in the sense that practice and hence real building tends to play with more than one image at a time, as we shall discuss later. This classification and tabling, of course, is the kind of act

Table 2.1 Three images of architectural sustainability

Image	Dominant concerns	Dominant horizon	Symbolism/aesthetics	Approach
Natural	Environmental place, ecosystems, health, balance	Local	'Touching the earth lightly' with forms echoing nature	Study local natural systems; emphasize sensitivity and humility in relation to nature.
Cultural	Cultural place, people, *genius loci*, difference, cultural sustainability	Local	Highly contextual with forms, materials and construction methods echoing the local vernacular	Study local culture and building; emphasize local involvement and local expertise
Technical	Technologies, global environmental impacts, cost-benefit analysis, risk management	Global	Leading edge contemporary international systems	Study science, economics and technology; emphasize transnational expertise

that modernists would do, and is yet another example of the ordering of discourse through listing and categorizing. Before looking at each of these categories in turn we shall make some general comments about the connections between images of sustainability and associated symbolism and aesthetics.

Architectural expression

In *The Ethical Function of Architecture*, Karsten Harries (1997) addresses architecture's task of helping to articulate a common ethos, to interpret a way of life for our period. He is concerned with both the actual and 'rhetorical' (visually indicated) function of buildings, and the associated roles of aesthetics and what he terms the 'problem' of architectural language, when those who view a building do not understand the secondary meanings of its language. This 'problem' refers to the way in which the particular form and details of a building are meaningful only to those who understand the cultural and functional reasoning behind them. Ultimately, we can only fully understand a building by being a part of the community that builds it, with its values (and perhaps not even then). Thus we cannot design a building to fully reflect a regional culture which we do not share. We can, though, seek to reflect our (admittedly partial) understanding and values of architectural sustainability. This symbolic dimension is desirable and necessary, and the recognition and invention of accepted symbols has always been a part of architecture. Architects are inevitably interested in the tectonic potential of the forms that can arise with a sound understanding of sustainability and ecology, and what this will suggest and privilege in building form, materials and decoration.

In the late nineteenth and early twentieth centuries, chimneys were often emphasized as elements in design compositions – note, for example, the importance of chimneys in the aesthetics of houses designed by Edwin Lutyens in England or Frank Lloyd Wright in America. Chimneys were essential to the functioning of houses, and styles developed where they were integral and necessary to the style. Sunshades, cooling shafts, solar panels and rammed earth walls – and other features – are exploited as design elements in contemporary buildings, so that the architectural expression of these features becomes a significant part of the aesthetics and character of the building (Baird 2001). This is 'form follows function' in the tradition of modernism, with its commitment to derive beautiful form directly from function. The aesthetic qualities of the building are justified and rationalized because they are expressions of its environmental functions and the conditions of its production, as in nature.[7] This imparts a sense of legitimacy and conviction to the appearance, a sense that has been neither sought nor demonstrated in much postmodern architecture, with its justification of form and decoration on other grounds of coding and meaning.[8] But in the same way that the buildings of modernism are sometimes criticized for functions that appear to have been invented to justify the aesthetics, there are doubtless cases where the desire to make form with towers or shades has driven the decision to adopt corresponding 'environmental' devices, rather than vice versa.

So where is the boundary between a 'legitimate' symbol of sustainability, and the proliferation of ecogadgets as a feature of greenwash that was noted in Chapter 1? And where is the boundary between a respectful learning from a local vernacular and the cynical use of cultureclamps? Symbolization is a profound human need and is indispensable for the perpetuation of culture. The symbol accentuates the presence of a building which has genuine and reasoned claims to be in some ways 'more sustainable' than most of its contemporaries. It can raise questions in those who occupy and see the building – how and why does this place 'work'? Why is sustainability important? Greenwash and culturewash are counterfeit or disguise – or simply a demonstration of lack of knowledge, which in turn may demonstrate lack of real concern.

The natural image

In his enormously influential book *Design with Nature*, published in 1969, Ian McHarg argues that

> If one accepts the simple proposition that nature is the arena of life and that a modicum of knowledge of her processes is indispensable for survival and rather more for existence, health and delight, it is amazing how many apparently difficult problems present ready solution.
>
> (McHarg 1969: 7)

In the natural image, the key to architectural sustainability is to work *with*, not *against*, nature; to understand, sensitively exploit and simultaneously avoid damaging natural systems. As a planner and landscape architect, McHarg used examples from regional planning in identifying places with intrinsic suitability for agriculture, forestry, recreation and urbanization. 'Design with nature' at the building level is a code for recognizing sun paths, breezes, shade trees and rock formations as natural features that can be 'worked with' in making somewhere for people to inhabit, while recognizing significant trees, animal tracks, habitats and natural drainage systems as natural features that must be 'protected'. When seeking a device with a high shading coefficient in summer and a low coefficient in winter, a vine may be used rather than a mechanical system; the vine shades the building when (and only when) it is needed, and the building provides a 'home' for the vine. Thus both the building and the 'other' of nature are sustainable. By adding rainwater collection, reed beds for sewage and perhaps wind or solar power for electrical energy the building 'working with nature' can be independent of imported services and exported waste, keeping its environmental footprint within the footprint of its site. The archetypal visual image is the remote and isolated self-sufficient building dominated by its surrounding landscape.

The natural image of architectural sustainability, then, mirrors a view that it is necessary to position human activities as a non-damaging part of the ongoing ecological landscape, with a belief that 'nature knows best'. The 'eco-centric' logic that Guy and Farmer (2001: 142–3) identify in the discourse of architecture embraces this image of sustainability, linking it strongly with a rhetoric of a fragile, delicately balanced earth where straying far from this path will lead to environmental catastrophe. Even if that is the way it occurs in contemporary writing, the natural image has a currency and attraction without this threat of doom. Frank Lloyd Wright, after all, published *The Natural House* in 1954.[9] Two other logics that Guy and Farmer report in the discourse of architecture are also linked to this natural image, the 'eco-medical' logic and the 'eco-aesthetic' logic. The former encompasses a discourse focusing on healthy people in 'healthy' buildings, drinking 'pure' water and breathing 'clean' air. The natural image *naturally* assumes purity in the environment, because pristine nature is unblemished by the act of building. Moreover, the calming and stress-free attributes attributed to nature[10] are also encompassed in this image, so that mental health accompanies physical health: a healthy mind in a healthy body in a healthy building, in which humans and other creatures live in happy harmony.

2.2 The natural image: 'Hollow Spruce' (1988) in Grizedale Forest, England, artist Richard Harris (photographer Richard Harris).

The symbolic and 'eco-aesthetic' manifestations of this image reinforce identification with nature and natural systems.[11] Materials are those of nature with little human modification: straw bale, rammed earth and pressed mud brick, or rough-hewn stone, and 'natural' timber rather than 'manufactured' timber particle boards, all with 'natural' finishes. Soft, organic, sensuous curves may be favoured over hard mechanical angles, and 'earth colours' over brighter hues. Neither does the building dominate its natural setting. Rather it expresses humility in the face of nature, its character coming as much from the play of sunlight and shade over its surface as from its own form. This move from the clearly artificial towards immersion in the subtleties, folds, movement and restraint of nature brings to mind the parallel movement in environmental art. Indeed, for an emblem of the natural image we can turn to art. Richard Harris's literally and metaphorically organic 'Hollow Spruce' (1988) in Grizedale Forest in the Lake District of northern England (Figure 2.2) 'acts as a filter through which to re-experience the light, sound, colour and space of the dense Spruce' (Harris 1991: 49).[12] An impression of shelter (of a kind) is provided, but it is constructed of local materials with minimal impact on its environment and will decay back into the same environment. Even the fact that we can see that to inhabit this 'building' would necessitate giving up much of our expectations of personal comfort is a part of the natural image. We are prepared to do so for the benefits to us of 'living close to nature' and the benefits to nature of continuing to live undisturbed. But with care, 'designing with nature' can provide both physical and spiritual comfort (Day 2000). Like its occupants, the building lives in happy harmony with its setting.

The cultural image

In *Architecture: Meaning and Place*, Christian Norberg-Schulz laments the way that place and artefacts have lost meaning for 'modern man':

> In general, the loss of things and places makes up a loss of 'world'. Modern man becomes 'worldless', and thus loses his own identity, as well as the sense of community and participation. Existence is experienced as 'meaningless,' and man becomes 'homeless' because he does not any longer belong to a meaningful totality. Moreover he becomes 'careless,' since he does not feel the urge to protect and cultivate a world any more.
>
> (Norberg-Schulz 1988: 12)

The cultural image portrays a distinct and meaningful *genius loci* of which architecture is a part. It mirrors an anthropological view that promotes keeping people culturally in place, combined with a belief that 'the local culture knows best'. Sustainability means protecting and continuing this *genius loci*, and working within the limitations and possibilities that this requires. Sustainability of the building is sublimated to sustainability of the place. The image embraces a concern for the way local people live and interact with their buildings, and an expectation that this will be different from other places.

The symbolic and aesthetic manifestations of the image reinforce identification with 'authentic place' and celebrate discernible difference between places. Since the local vernacular mode of building is seen as having authentically emerged as a response to local culture and the *genius loci* (and, indeed, to be an important part of that culture), it is the model for new building. Materials, colours and building forms draw on this local vernacular. Buildings are highly contextual, following Christopher Alexander's notion in *A New Theory of Urban Design* (1987) of new development as 'healing the city', of repairing wherever the 'authentic place' is damaged by earlier inappropriate work. But new building also symbolizes the continuing vitality of the local culture, so that the new building is expected to rework rather than reproduce the vernacular, to be identifiably contemporary while eminently respectful of the past.

An emblem of the cultural image might be the Mosque at New Gourna (1945) designed by Hassan Fathy to recognize traditional Nubian vernacular forms. Fathy set out to create buildings in 'a style that he believed incorporated the essence of his own culture' (Steele, 1997: 6), informed by and respecting tradition but not simply reproducing it. The main façade of the mosque (Figure 2.3) 'uses a very sophisticated and deliberate kind of iconography' combining elements with complex historical connotations that are regional but also 'transcend local tradition to make a connection with the formation of Islamic identity itself'

2.3 The vernacular image: The Mosque at New Gourna, Egypt (1945), architect Hassan Fathy, built with forms and materials echoing the local vernacular (photographer Barry Rowney).

(Steele 1997: 75). New Gourna is his best-known community project, built to relocate the village of Gourna al-Gadida to be more distant from the famous tombs in the Valleys of the Kings, Queens and Nobles in Luxor.[13] Steele notes six principles that guided Fathy: humanism, a universal approach, appropriate technology (mud brick in the Mosque, as in the local vernacular), socially orientated construction techniques, tradition, and 'the reestablishment of national cultural pride through the act of building' (Steele 1997: 16).

The impression that it would be difficult to expand this architectural language to accommodate the diversity and scale of contemporary requirements is a part of the cultural image. In it we have to accept that sustaining culture may mean limiting what is accommodated (the insertion of new activities into the community) as well as how buildings look.

The 'eco-cultural' and 'eco-social' logics which Guy and Farmer identify both overlap this cultural image. The discourse of the 'eco-cultural' logic frames local ecology and climate as a part of the sense of place, helping to define the culture and vernacular. The discourse of the 'eco-social' logic 'suggests the creation of buildings that embody and express the notion of a social and ecological community in which democratic values such as full participation and freedom is the norm' (Guy and Farmer 2001: 146). In the idealized vernacular image, the identifiable community is assumed to be healthy, democratic and self-sufficient with a clear sense of identity and belonging: happy people living in happy cooperation with one another. Like the people, the buildings cooperate with each other in collectively making a place with an equally clear sense of identity and difference.

The technical image

In an interview about his design work for the Reichstag parliament building in Berlin, the architect Lord Norman Foster said:

> Since Stonehenge, architects have always been at the cutting edge of technology. And you can't separate technology from the humanistic and spiritual content of a building . . . This building is highly engineered . . . great mirrors bring light down right into the debating chamber . . . It looks forward to the day when buildings will give off no pollution, no greenhouse gases.
>
> (Foster 1999)

The technical image of sustainability portrays technical innovation in the solution of social, economic and environmental problems. In this image sustainability is a matter of developing technical devices that neutralize or make benefits out of what may temporarily appear to be problems. The track record of architects over the centuries in finding technical solutions to innumerable problems inspires confidence that the same will happen in the future. Success is seen as a matter of applying the tools of the social, economic and physical sciences to analyse the situation and discover a range of answers. But neither applying these tools nor implementing the answers is easy. The prerequisite for success is professional expertise.

The technical image forefronts hard 'facts', and particularly the measurable 'environmental facts' of the constituents of air, lighting and noise levels, resource consumption, etc., along with equally measurable economics. Success can also be measured: reduced energy consumption, reduced embodied energy in materials, internal temperatures and lighting levels within desired levels, reduced initial and operating costs. The key is rationality and efficiency in planning, material use and systems.

The symbolic/aesthetic representation of the image is one of technical proficiency in using the materials of contemporary architecture: sparkling glass, gleaming stainless steel, precision cladding panels in alloys or aluminium (justified by their low weight and long life). Passive and active devices such as double skin external walls and roofs, filtering and responsive glass, 'sun scoops', sun-tracking sunshades and photovoltaic panels supplement this international language of architecture. Not visible will be geothermal systems, heat recovery, and the 'intelligent' computer control of lighting, heating and cooling via timers and movement detectors. The archetypal visual image is the high-tech corporate office in a city of similar offices: efficient people in efficient buildings, both in control, both responding to challenges through innovation. An emblematic project might be the Commerzbank Headquarters in Frankfurt, Germany (architects Foster and Partners), described as 'the world's first ecological high-rise office block'[14] and, when constructed, Europe's tallest building (Figure 2.4). It has many technical features. Amongst them are double skin walls, dual natural and artificial ventilation systems (openable windows which can all be closed by a central control, with natural ventilation replaced by full air conditioning when weather conditions dictate), four-storey high winter gardens which enable inward-facing offices to have natural light, an atrium acting as a ventilation chimney, and sludge water from the air-conditioning cooling towers used for flushing lavatories (Jones 1998: 228; Daniels 1995: 91–5). But we could also adopt as an emblematic project a small house or a factory. Indeed, the facilities for the 2000 Olympic Games in Sydney, Australia, hailed for the environmental responsibility that was a factor in the original award of the Games to Sydney in a highly competitive bid process, overwhelmingly reinforce the technology image. It is a part of this image that technology can deal with *any* project in *any* place.

The 'eco-technic' logic that Guy and Farmer (2001: 142) find in the discourse of architectural sustainability projects this image. They note its link to 'ecological modernization' at the policy level, which portrays apparently serious environmental side-effects of development as just more problems in the path of modernization which can be managed, like other problems, by international treaties and local regulation. The field of significance is global, the problems are global (with an emphasis on climate change and transnational pollution), and the answers and the expertise to implement them are universally applicable.

2.4 The technology image: Commerzbank Headquarters, Frankfurt, Germany, 1997, architects Foster Associates, contrasting with old city buildings (photographer Ian Lambot).

Overlapping images

These three images have been implicitly presented as corners of a triangle. The discourse, as Guy and Farmer report, is centred on the image that is dominant and structures sustainability into narrower domains than we do here. But if we look at buildings, including regional vernaculars (Figure 2.5), we are likely to find two or all of our three images reflected to varying degrees.

Architects play many games at once, using many images. Thus the little Carey Gully house (1989–96), (Figure 2.6) in the Adelaide Hills of Australia

2.5 The vernacular embodying overlapping images of sustainability: House in the Sigatoka Valley on the Pacific island of Fiji under construction in 1979. Unmodified 'natural' materials characterize traditional local building using a technology of tied wood and bamboo frame, woven grass walls and thatched roof (photographer Antony Radford).

(architects Grose Bradley) has mud brick and corrugated iron walls (cultural image) in a curvilinear form derived from the sun path (natural image) with solar panels perched on top of a steel-framed tower (technology image). Behind the walls is a composting toilet and beside the house is a rainwater tank with a footprint almost as big as the house. Even 'Hollow Spruce', our emblem of the natural image, has its contemporary technology. Richard Harris wrote 'I found an inner tube from a tractor tyre near to my site, and cut it into strips to tie the branches together'.[15] The use of mud bricks in the Mosque at New Gourna alludes to natural and technological as well as cultural images. Commerzbank, our emblem of the technology image, seeks to make the most of natural systems and reflects the contemporary cultures of its place and production.

We shall cite three other office buildings to illustrate different emphasis in their combinations of images. Eastgate (Figure 2.7) in Harare, Zimbabwe, 1996 by architects Pearce Partnership is a large mixed office and retail development. It demonstrates the established rational 'building as environmental system' approaches of the technology image: stack effects, fans, heat transfer through a maze of precast concrete elements (Baird 2001: 164–80, Jones 1998: 200–1). It sets out to work with the specifics of the local climate as in the natural image, particularly the cool, clear nights which facilitate heat loss overnight by convection and radiation. It also manages to suggest the culturally-specific 'definable

2.6 Carey Gully House, South Australia, 1989–96, architects Grose Bradley (photographer Antony Radford).

difference' of the cultural image. The row of chimneys along the roof, the deep recessing of windows, and the depth of double floors in the offices are all expressed strongly as tectonic elements.

The 'bioclimatic skyscrapers'[16] of Ken Yeang (T. R. Hamzah and Yeang) exhibit organic form and the extensive use of planting as 'vertical landscaping'[17] recreating 'ground conditions in the sky' (Yeang 1995). These reflect the natural image, achieved with an architectural language and use of devices associated

2.7 Eastgate mixed shop and office building, Harare, Zimbabwe, 1996, architects Pearce Partnership (photographer George Baird).

with the technology image. Yeang's series of skyscraper projects are committed experiments in a reflective practice (Schön 1982) seeking high performance combined with low embodied and operating energy through passive techniques responding to climate. The EDITT Tower, Figure 2.8, in Singapore (competition design 1998) is an exemplar of the 'bioclimatic skyscraper'. It adopts many climate responsive techniques: 'wind walls' to direct wind to internal spaces, solar panels, mechanically-joined connections between building components to facilitate recycling, rainwater collection, sewage composting, and grey-water re-use. Vegetation in the 'vertical landscaping' spirals upwards from street level

2.8 EDITT (Ecological Design in The Tropics) Tower, Singapore (model of 1998 competition design), architects T. R. Hamzah & Yeang Sdn Bhd.

in a linked landscape ramp, with street activities (including stalls and shops) lining the ramp for the first six floors.[18]

Walter Dobkins' design for the Comesa Centre,[19] Lusaka, Zambia (1990–94) connects aesthetics, sustainability, appropriate technology and the building's multiple cultural contexts (Figures 2.9, 2.10). Dobkins says he did not set out to make a 'statement' about ecology or culture: 'I wasn't trying to design a building with or for alternative technology. I wanted a 'people-friendly' building.'[20] He merely responded in straightforward ways to the realities of building in Lusaka at the time. Part of this reality is the truism that the lower technology, the less there is to go wrong. The building is low-rise so that elevators are unnecessary (there is ramp access to the upper floors via an adjacent car park, hardly ideal access for disabled people but reliable), and it avoids air conditioning (as far as the client and computer technology would allow). Apart from the banking hall, the plan is arranged as narrow wings, each with a single bank of offices to facilitate day lighting and cross-ventilation. An open corridor on the sunny side provides shading, and windows are split horizontally so that the upper part can

2.9 Comesa Centre (previously Meridien Centre) main hall, Lusaka, Zambia, 1994, architect Walter Dobkins (photographer Ian Murphy).

2.10 Comesa Centre, between two wings (photographer Ian Murphy).

be opened with the lower part closed to prevent papers blowing about in windy conditions.[21] Materials are local: slate floors using the random slates offered by a 'cottage' industry alongside the roads leading into Lusaka, cut into squares on site; rendered walls of concrete blocks made on site; timber trusses made up from dark-stained 'tree trunk' timber members joined by hand-made steel connectors and locally-made concrete roof tiles. While these are all sensible choices in an African context, they are not the choices made in most comparable buildings either in Africa or in other parts of the world. All the choices have aesthetic implications, and Dobkins works them into an aesthetic result that is (to the Western eye) gently evocative of traditional Zambian building.

In this chapter we have looked at how the discourse of architecture and the work of architects reveals 'where we seem to be' as a profession and discipline. Taken together, the images of sustainability portray a rich, diverse and contested picture. They display what Pérez-Gómez suggests is 'the fundamental paradox of the modern world' with its

> Simultaneous belief in reason (with its infinite capacity to discover absolutely certain mathematical facts) and the belief in the radical subjectivity of each human being, condemned to his own partial perspective of the world (providing only a limited access to 'objective' reality).
>
> (Pérez-Gómez 1983: 274)

But whom or what are we working for, in the sense of who and what are the stakeholders on whose behalf we are making design decisions in making a building? Is it the client or the planet, or both, or some less easily defined collection of entities? In the next chapter we shall explore how ethics and ethical positions underlie the recognition of stakeholders in the development process, and through this recognition fundamentally affect the understanding of appropriate goals and outcomes for that process. This, in turn, may lead us to lean towards (or help explain why we may lean towards) a particular image of sustainable architecture.

Notes

1 Christian Norberg-Schulz has written about these issues in architecture; see Norberg-Schulz, 1988 p. 11 and following *Architecture: Meaning and Place*, Electa/Rizzoli, New York, 1988.

2 The exhibition *Architecture Without Architects* was shown at the Museum of Modern Art, New York, in 1964–65.

3 Differences between the ways in which the indigenous people and later immigrants to these countries view value and 'rights' of elements of the natural landscape have led to continuing and unresolved conflict between those who see the land in terms of ownership (legal rights of occupation) and those who see it in terms of self identity.

4 A description of image theory is provided by Lee Roy Beach in his book, *Image Theory: Decision Making in Personal and Organizational Contexts* (1990). He differentiates between mental and cognitive images:

> *Mental images* are psychologically (centrally) generated quasi-pictorial events . . . For example, you can call to mind your mother's face . . . Moreover, these images can be mentally manipulated – imagine your mother starting to frown and then breaking into a big smile. . . . *Cognitive images* . . . are a combination of mental image and non-image knowledge. That is, cognitive images have some features that are pictorial, some that are semantic and some that are emotional (for surely emotions must be regarded as a form of knowledge).
>
> (Beach 1990: 16–17)

These definitions may be useful for indicating the scope of images rather than drawing clear distinctions between them as, in practice, it is difficult to determine when an image is 'mental' rather than 'cognitive' and writers frequently use the term 'mental image' in ways that suggest both of these types. Frances Downing defines a mental image as

> The sensation of environmental phenomena through vision, movement, sound, smell, or taste, captured and held in abeyance for moments of time in the mind of an individual. . . . A mental image helps codify and order the endlessly complex world of human experience.
>
> (Downing 1992b: 442)

Elsewhere Downing says:

> Mental images are an active, vital repository of information gathered through sensual experience – through sight, sound, smell, touch, and taste. A mental image presents more than an initial remembered precept to the mind; it contains multiple versions of involvement that stretch beyond the experiential to the emotional and intellectual realms.
>
> (Downing 1994: 235)

5 Amartya Sen in a lecture called *Global Doubts as Global Solutions* referred to Sanskrit texts in India, beginning about 2500 years ago, warning us not to be 'well frogs'. These are creatures that live in wells, and therefore have a single well-defined (pun intended) horizon and world view. He mischievously suggested that 'there are plenty of "well frogs" around today' (Deakin Lecture, Melbourne Town Hall, Australia, 15 May 2001).

6 'Today architects work under the absurd assumption that meaning and symbol are merely products of the mind, that they can be manufactured a priori and that they possess somehow the certainty of number' (Pérez-Gómez 1983: 12).

7 Nature has long been used as a model in claiming that function, form and beauty are interconnected. Horatio Greenhough (1805–1852) wrote a series of essays that were collected and republished under the title *Form and Function* in 1947. He notes connections between beauty, action and character as phases of 'natural' life:

> When I define Beauty as the promise of function; Action as the presence of Function; Character as the record of Function, I arbitrarily divide that which is essentially one. . . . Beauty, being the promise of function, must be mainly present before the phase of action; but so long as there is yet a promise of function there is beauty, proportioned to its relation with action or with character.

He criticized then-contemporary American architecture for seeking beauty through formalism and applied decoration (Greenhough 1947: 71). Earlier, Durand had argued in the *Précis des leçons d'architecture* (1802) that 'no architecture decoration would be pleasant . . . unless it sprang from the most convenient and economical "disposition" '. 'Here is the direct precedent of twentieth-century functionalism, which is still present today in explicit and disguised forms' (Pérez-Gómez 1983: 299).

8   See Spector (2001: 45) for a brief summary.
9   *The Natural House* focuses on Wright's 'Usonian' houses'. The dust jacket of a 1971
    edition published by Pitman, London, quotes Wright:

> The Usonian house aims to be a *natural* performance, one that is integral to site,
> to environment, to the life of the inhabitants, integral with the nature of
> materials . . . into this new integrity, once there, those that live in it will take
> root and grow.' Wright writes: 'Nature is the great teacher – man can only receive
> and respond to her teaching.
>
> (Wright 1971: 186)

10 We know that 'Nature' as it operates can be brutal, but we still retain an image of
    tranquillity.
11 While 'architecture is ecological only if it fulfils certain objective demands in rela-
    tion to nature' (von Bonsdorff 1993: 9), this is not enough. 'An ecological architec-
    ture should be more than that: a communication and affirmation of ecological values'
    (von Bonsdorff 1993: 6). Further, 'If ecology were only a question of finding the right
    ways to interact with nature, ecological architecture would be a less intriguing con-
    cept. As it is, ecology is also a cultural concept . . .' (von Bonsdorff 1993: 8).
12 In fact the branches are waste product from renewable plantation forest – also symbolic.
13 New Gourna in 2002 is a place where later buildings with little sense of 'cultural
    place' surround Fathy's work. Moreover, people still live amongst the tombs; the
    economy centred on the tombs (guards, tourist guides and vendors) as well as con-
    tinuity of dwelling all support their choice, and population growth means plenty of
    people to occupy both 'new' and 'old' Gourna.
14 The claim is reported in Jones (1998: 228). It is made (probably amongst other places)
    in Thirty Years: Foster and Partners (CD), Foster and Partners, London, 1998.
15 Harris comments that 'The inner tube . . . seemed to be as apt as most of the forest,
    which is made up largely of non-native species' (Harris 1991: 50).

16   We can define the bioclimatic skyscraper as a tall building whose built form is
       configured by design, using passive low-energy techniques to relate to the site's
       climate and meteorological data, resulting in a tall building that is environment-
       ally interactive, low energy in embodiment and operations, and high quality in
       performance.

       (Yeang 1996: 18)

Yeang's work is reviewed in Powell (1999).

17   Traditionally, landscape planting is laced horizontally. However, in the case of
       the tall building, a vertical approach or 'vertical landscaping' is needed. Vertical
       landscaping is simply plant and other organic material integrated vertically with
       the tall building.

       (Yeang 1995: 101)

18 The clients (sponsors) were the Urban Redevelopment Authority, EDITT (Ecological
    Design in the Tropics), and the National University of Singapore. Information about
    the project was provided by T. R. Hamzah & Yeang Sdn Bhd, architects, March 2002.
19 Originally the Meridien Centre.
20 Dobkins, personal communication, January 1995.
21 Dobkins comments on the influence of culture on the environmental operation of
    the building: employees 'tend not to open windows, but to work with the blinds
    down and the lights on' despite the inevitable lesser physical comfort (personal
    communication, January 1995).

3 Ethics

Ethics is essentially a practical matter. It is concerned with how we should live, how we should treat other people and the world around us, in short, how we should act in a moral and responsible manner. Most opinions or appeals to act in a certain way that include an 'ought' or 'should' are normative ethical claims. These normative views and beliefs attempt to prescribe behaviour; for example, 'Wilderness areas ought to be protected', 'Heritage buildings should be preserved', 'Buildings should be designed to have less reliance on non-renewable fossil fuels', and 'Carbon dioxide emissions should be diminished'. Clearly the entreaties to embrace notions of sustainability and a sustainable architecture have ethical dimensions, but how is the architect to respond? Typical professional moral behaviour is expressed in terms of guidelines, rules, standards and codes. As Tom Spector observes, 'the nature of building codes reinforces the idea that professional moral obligations exist within a network of well-defined relationships, expectations, and activities' (Spector 2001: 130).

Relying on this conventional mode of responsible decision-making to achieve a truly sustainable architecture is problematic. The issues and requirements for a sustainable architecture are likely to extend beyond a reliance on existing conventions and empirical knowledge, and will require strategies over and above the legal obligations of complying with planning regulations and building codes.

Seeking guidance on responsible decision-making in terms of ethical codes of practice and standards has also been criticized as a modernist project aimed at shifting moral responsibility away from the self with the well intentioned, but impossible, aim of constructing a world free of moral uncertainty.[1] If this is true (as it would appear to be) then we need to ask 'can guidance be found from another source?' Foucault, for example, seems to suggest that 'taking care of oneself' is a precondition for sustainability. 'A city in which everyone took proper care of himself would be a city that functioned well and found in this the ethical principle of its permanence' (Foucault 1997: 287). While this 'taking care of oneself' also implies taking care of others and the world around us, how can we be guided in such a quest, especially when we realize that as architects we run the risk of imposing our own fantasies, appetites, and desires on others?

3.1 Human intervention in 'unspoilt nature': a walkers' hut in the Cradle Mountain World Heritage wilderness area, Tasmania, Australia, architect Ken Latona (photographer Simon Kenny).

We can begin to tackle this question by realizing that our programme to understand (if only partly) the dimensions of the concept of a sustainable architecture is integrally linked to the belief systems that generate the notion itself. Taking this as a starting point, we can confront the questions about the ethical or moral bases of our decision-making.[2] We shall present in barest outline reasons and motives that can explain good and wrong decisions. This is tackled in two ways. The first looks at why decisions are made according to certain ethical precepts, focusing on the question 'Just who or what could (or should) be taken into consideration as a stakeholder in responsible decision-making?' This investigation raises issues that are at the forefront when making ethical judgements – the meaning and use of the term value, the rights of humans (or other members of a moral class who are held to have rights), the duties we might have to respect such rights, and understanding the consequences of actions. The second looks at how decisions are made and focuses on the spectrum of two broad approaches we might invoke to understand ethical processes in action – environmental ethics, in particular the way in which we position humans and other stakeholders in sustainability issues, and discursive ethics, as 'a process of uncoerced and undistorted communicative interaction between individuals in open discourse' that can provide an operational means of informing ethical behaviour (O'Hara 1996).

Questions about value

Since most attempts at ethical reasoning develop from a consideration of the notion of value, and questions of value are central to the discussion of sustainability, we will begin our examination at this point.[3] Des Jardins observes that 'a full account of value determines the ethical domain by helping to define what objects have moral relevance or what objects deserve consideration'. But what do we mean when we talk about something or some state of affairs as being valuable? What is value? How does value arise? Philosophers, economists and of course environmentalists are endlessly discussing (and hotly disputing) these sorts of questions.[4] They are crucial in understanding the debates and predicaments associated with making sustainable architecture.

If we start by accepting that humans have a right to life and freedom that may not be infringed, then these are of central value. Aristotle (fourth century BC) in the first major treatise on ethics in Western philosophy attributes to *happiness*, meaning human good, the greatest human value and its pursuit as the self-evident goal for moral decision-making. Happiness for Aristotle was the conjunction of an aesthetic component to be 'sufficiently equipped with external goods' and virtuous activity, 'activity in accordance with complete virtue' (Aristotle 1962: 1, 1101a). Moral behaviour for him turns out to be 'an activity of the soul in conformity with excellence or virtue' (Aristotle 1962: 1, 1098a). For utilitarians like Jeremy Bentham (1748–1832) and John Stuart Mill (1806–1873), *happiness* is again clearly the key value. In this case *happiness* turns more on the aesthetic element and has a meaning more akin to what we may regard as pleasure. Their attitudes, fostered by the eighteenth-century Enlightenment project, promoted the idea that decision-making should consider the social utility to maximize happiness and minimize pain. More recently, the moral philosopher Kurt Baier in his investigation of *What is Value? An Analysis of the Concept* draws attention to the difference between 'the *value* possessed by things' and the '*values* held by people or societies'. He sees that:

> The former is an evaluative property whose possession and magnitude can be ascertained in appraisals. The latter are dispositions to behave in certain ways which can be ascertained by observation. The former are capacities of things to satisfy desiderata. The latter are tendencies of people to devote their resources (time, energy, money) to attainment of certain ends.
>
> (Baier 1969: 40)

In both these cases the value is contingent upon some factor of utility, that is, the value is *instrumental*. To economists the 'values held by people or societies' are expressed as preferences to act in certain ways. For Baier *non-instrumental* or *intrinsic* value is always relegated to a secondary role of consideration.[5] Many environmental ethicists now totally disagree with such assertions and believe that landscapes, other organisms, and ecosystems may in some way have an intrinsic value that is just as important (or perhaps more important) than other values. Des Jardins explains that,

> To say that an object is intrinsically valuable is to say that it has a good of its own and what is good for it does not depend on outside factors. In this sense, it would be a value found or recognized rather than given.
>
> (Des Jardins 2001: 133)

This distinction is of particular importance to our understanding of sustainability ethics, where questions about the value of the natural versus the constructed worlds are central to decision-making. The problem faced by a local council when considering a development application illustrates this point. Imagine a popular, beautiful tourist spot near a country town. The council is under considerable pressure to approve a second café to cater for tourists. Both the proposed developers and a coalition of local residents and environmentalists opposing the development describe the place and its landscape as valuable – but what do they mean by *valuable* (in this case there must be obvious differences in interpretation) and why do they see it as valuable?

We can begin by citing a number of instances in which this place has instrumental value to human beings. Many people value it as a place to pursue leisure activities, going for a walk, as somewhere to view wildlife, or as a splendid location in which to paint or photograph. We might value it because we appreciate the aesthetic qualities of its scenery, indigenous peoples might see it as a place with strong spiritual and ancestral connections, and for the existing café owner it is an opportunity to make money. Certain animals also find it useful – perhaps rare birds build their nests there. All these examples are instances illustrating instrumental value. But can we also say that the place has non-instrumental or intrinsic value? Can this intrinsic value be something of itself or is it something imagined by humans?

This divergence in understanding is seen as a difference between value subjectivists and value objectivists. Value subjectivists argue that intrinsic value is an entity created by humans and attached to the object of consideration. Value objectivists, on the other hand, believe that intrinsic value is *not* something humans create but something that is integral to the world around us. They argue that they are not creating value but rather recognizing the value of the place already present, value that would continue to exist even if there were no human beings to value it.

Maintaining an objectivist view has some logical difficulties when faced with certain questions. For example: 'Is the value of objects or individuals a property they possess, rather like their weight?', 'What if people disagree (as they do) over how much objects or individuals might have of this property?', and 'How can we decide who is right?' Dealing with these questions is less awkward for those who may believe in a God, at least in the Judaeo-Christian tradition. For them, since God created the world and saw that it was good, humans can recognize and value God's work and understand that every aspect of the world was created for a purpose.[6] Fulfilling this purpose provides a *natural law* basis for judging ethical behaviour. Francis of Assisi worshipped all aspects of nature for this reason and is considered by some to be the patron saint of ecologists. Human responsibility for the Earth is interpreted as one of stewardship with a duty to God, and through this a responsibility to the rest of creation who represent God. HRH The Prince of Wales in his 2000 BBC Reith lecture emphasized this duty of stewardship:

> The idea that there is a sacred trust between mankind and our Creator, under which we accept a duty of stewardship for the Earth, has been an important feature of most religious and spiritual thought throughout the ages.
>
> (HRH The Prince of Wales 2000)

Sir John Houghton, the chairman of the John Ray Institute that promotes responsible environmental stewardship in accordance with Christian principles, (he is also co-chairman of the Scientific Assessment Working Group for the Intergovernmental Panel on Climate Change, and a member of the UK Government Panel on Sustainable Development), goes a step further and suggests that 'the disasters we find everywhere in the environment speak eloquently' of a broken relationship with God as a result of human sin:

> When thinking of the sin and evil which results from a broken relationship with God, Christians generally think of sin against people not against the environment. But if we take seriously the clear responsibility of care for the Earth given to humans by God, we are bound also to recognise that to fail

in that task is not only a sin against nature but a sin against God. It has been suggested that this new category of sin should include activities that lead to 'species extinction, reduction in genetic diversity, pollution of the water, land and air, habitat destruction and disruption of sustainable life styles'. This new sense of sin could also include the sin of too much talk and too little action!

(Houghton 1998)

But for those who do not hold that ethics has a theological basis, it is more difficult to explain the nature of objective value and where it might come from. René Dubos in his book *A God Within* offers an alternative account combining elements of both subjective and objective views:

> The various microcosms, or ecosystems, with which man deals are his own mental creations; indeed they derive their size and shape from the characteristics and limitations of his senses and conceptual apparatus. The 'spirit' or 'genius' of a place, of a creature, or of an object, is the perception of some facet of nature by the god within the human observer.

(Dubos 1976: 19)

He argues the need to nurture the intrinsic values that exist both in each person and in our external worlds. But if something – a person, an animal, a landscape – has value (instrumental or intrinsic), does it also have rights? If so, whether or not such rights should be taken into account in making responsible decisions is a key consideration in thinking about sustainability.

The moral class

A key set of issues in dealing with the ethical dimensions of sustainability are those that take in the question 'who is due moral consideration?', or put another way related more directly to the question of a sustainable architecture – 'who (or what) are the members of the moral class who should be regarded as stakeholders in our design decisions?' While Aristotle's ethics was concerned with the question 'what kind of person should I be', a major thread in Western philosophical tradition from Thomas Aquinas through Immanuel Kant until the present times is concerned with the question 'what sort of rules should I follow': what should guide our conduct towards each other, our behaviour towards others and, at the same time, the others' behaviour towards us? In this tradition aspects of sustainability such as resource usage, pollution, species extinction and landscape degradation are addressed only to the extent that they impinge on the well-being or assets of ourselves or other humans. If this is the limit of our concern, how can a notion of sustainability that also incorporates extending the concept of moral standing to future generations of humans be justified? We will see this is not entirely a straightforward issue.

The totally anthropocentric view of moral considerability that persisted for about 2500 years has been challenged in the last twenty-five years or so.

Table 3.1 Membership of the moral class

Membership of the moral class	*Criterion for membership*	*General orientation*
Humans	'Soul', rationality	Anthropocentric
Sentient creatures	Sentience (the power of perception by senses, capability for suffering)	Zoocentric, pathocentric
Animals and Plants	Life	Biocentric
Living, quasi-living and natural environments (includes natural objects such as mountains and rivers)	Holistic integrity and self-renewal	Ecocentric

Note
The rows are in order of extending inclusiveness, so that each row includes the membership of the row above.[8]

Environmental ethics considers a range of possible expansions and additions of what may be given moral standing, to include things other than human beings.[7] A systematic description of candidates for moral consideration are summarized in Table 3.1. But on what principles might we frame our actions and decisions towards this possible range of stakeholders? The ethical theories based on the notions of rights and duty provides an insight to this question.

Rights and duties

We are most familiar with the concept of human rights, reserved in common parlance for the political notions of equality before the law; protection against arbitrary arrest; the right to a fair trial; freedom of thought, conscience, and religion; freedom of opinion and expression and freedom of peaceful assembly and association. However, an appeal to respecting a wider notion of human rights may be seen as a basis for ethical decision-making. Certainly at both the international and domestic political level it is often put forward as the reason for action. Respecting human rights is closely associated with issues of sustainability:

> The history of the content of human rights also reflects humankind's recurring demands for continuity and stability. The right to political, economic, social, and cultural self-determination; the right to economic and social development; and the right to participate in and benefit from 'the common heritage of mankind' (shared Earth-space resources; scientific, technical, and other information and progress; and cultural traditions, sites, and monuments) . . . the right to peace, the right to a healthy and balanced environment.
>
> (Encyclopaedia Britannica 1998)

While we might all be familiar with this use of the word 'rights', how they arise and their exact nature is not entirely clear. We can take as an example 'the right to a standard of living adequate for health and well-being' as expressed in the *Universal Declaration of Human Rights*.[9] If you think that I have a right to *an adequate standard of living*, then you are accepting that you have a duty to ensure this happens, or at least not to contribute to anything that might infringe that right. Similarly if I think that you have a right to *an adequate standard of living*, I also accept a duty towards you. In this way rights and duties are correlated, and are different sides of the same coin. In a similar way human rights expressed in terms of *needs, wants and interests* that provide the basis of the standards and codes that guide the provision of buildings imply that we have a duty to respect these rights. The rise of Building Codes enshrines elements of respecting *basic* rights as a legal obligation. While Building Codes are ostensibly written to protect the health and safety rights of individuals, they also act in a wider sense to protect property rights and economic interests. On one hand they impose a duty to act in a certain way, and on the other they involve obligations not to interfere.

In another view of how rights might arise, they are seen as somewhat more fundamental and are granted to an entity that has an interest or a value (instrumental or intrinsic) that needs protection. In this view rights can be extended to all human and non-human entities (e.g. future generations, eco-systems, landscapes). A tree, for example, may be said to have a right to fulfil its potential to grow to its full height. Philosophers such as Alan White (White 1984) contest this view and suggest that if a right is something that one can enjoy, demand, claim, assert, waive, or surrender, then only those who can intelligibly be considered to exercise such actions can possess rights. It makes no sense therefore to say that an animal, or a tree or nature, or a future generation, has a right, although it may be deserving of serious consideration by those that do. White suggests that reasons for extending this consideration may often be supported by common sense, our shared moral values, the apparatus of law or some institutional system of regulations or conventions.

Because there is little consensus on how undisputed rights can arise, when it comes to ensuring responsible decision-making a better foundation is required. One such way of looking at the problem is to test the consistency of our actions. This implies that we have a duty to be consistent. We would be inconsistent, and therefore wrong, if in performing some action or making some decision we did exactly what we would disapprove of others doing. Designing a building so that it significantly reduced solar access for a neighbour's solar hot water heater (even if planning regulations did not prevent this) would be a wrong way to act because we would not want others to act in this way to us. This *golden rule* for moral behaviour is expressed in a general way as: if you don't want someone else to act in a certain way, then you shouldn't act in that way yourself. Perhaps 'environmental advocates' who regularly fly around the world thereby pouring greenhouse gases into the atmosphere, and who criticize others for doing the same thing, would be inconsistent in this sense.

A refined version of the golden rule was proposed by Immanuel Kant (1724–1804) who argued that humans have one fundamental ethical duty, that is, to treat other human beings as ends in themselves and not as means to an end. For Kant this principle must never be compromised whatever consequences could result (a very non-utilitarian perspective). This view has been particularly important in the development of ideas concerning decision-making on environmental issues. The focus of his test of ethical behaviour is based on a reasoned principle he termed the *categorical imperative*. While he formulates this in a number of ways, a general statement of the principle takes the form 'act only on that maxim through which you can at the same time will that it should become a universal law' (Feldman 1998: 185). A maxim is a motive for action expressed as a rule such as: 'Whenever I have the opportunity to design a building, I shall not concern myself with the consequences of the building on the society or on the environment other than issues covered by regulation (and where penalties exist for non-compliance)'. At first glance we might believe this attitude to be morally correct, but looking at the vast amount of literature on sustainable building design it is reasonable to presume that at least some architects believe this not to be a universal law, because in accepting it many aspects of design not the subject of regulation would be ignored. An attack on the maxim, and a demonstration that it is morally wrong, would go something like this. While we can cite aspects of aesthetic control, air quality, energy use and waste disposal where minimum requirements are the subject of planning or building codes, relatively few aspects of social and environmental impact of a building are in fact covered by regulation. The nature of the professional advice provided by an architect, however, is to inform the client fully of the implications of design decisions. Rarely do regulations, for example, deal with either design optimization or developing trade-off options beyond the minimum requirements. In the dynamic milieu that we now face, the social, environmental and economic consequences to be considered and taken into account are wide-ranging and reach further into the future than have been considered in the past. If an architect fails to investigate known issues they would be failing in a duty to their client. A universal failure (by all architects in following the maxim) would result in a loss in confidence of the profession and all architects would suffer. Because the maxim is not universalizable, to act that way is morally wrong. While some believe that introducing more and more regulations to cover all possible contingencies would eventually yield the correct result from the maxim, this hardly seems possible.

The rights/duty-based approach to ethics provides principles that carry weight out of proportion to the value of the consequences, that is, the approach tends to be absolute and cannot be abandoned, no matter what the circumstances. Ethical behaviour follows from respecting rights or fulfilling duties, rather than being driven by concern about the consequences of one's actions. However, another way to consider responsible decision-making is to focus on the consequences of one's actions.

The consequentialist approach

Consequentialist approaches to ethics are commonly followed in national policy-making and in personal decision-making. Consequentialist approaches contrast with the rights/duty-based approaches, because they are concerned with the consequences of actions rather than with the duties of the person acting. This approach is fundamentally linked to the concern of sustainability with considering the future consequences of present decisions.

Consequentialists hold that ethically correct behaviour is about producing the best consequences. If someone makes a decision based not on an expression of virtue, or the fulfilment of a duty, but rather because it is believed that better consequences will result from the action rather than from other possibilities, then this person is behaving in a consequentialist manner. What this means in practice is, however, far from simple. Best consequences depend on one's idea not only about the future but also about what is of value. The most usual answer to this question is associated with a school of consequentialist thought known as utilitarianism. The most influential utilitarian philosopher, John Stuart Mill, argued in his essay *Utilitarianism* that:

> The creed which accepts as the foundation of morals, Utility, or the Greatest Happiness Principle, holds that actions are right in proportion as they tend to promote happiness, wrong as they tend to produce the reverse of happiness. By happiness is intended pleasure, and the absence of pain; by unhappiness, pain, and the privation of pleasure . . .
>
> (Mill 1861)

Here, the best consequences are achieved by creating the greatest amount of happiness. Refinements to the consequentialist view see happiness as the satisfaction of desires or preferences because people are happy when they can get what they want or when as many individual preferences are satisfied as possible (Des Jardins 2001: 27). But whichever interpretation of best consequences is adopted, utilitarianism has further difficulties.

First, happiness, desires, or preferences are difficult to add up in order to assess the greatest amounts of them. Second, since utilitarians recognize no absolute rules (such as a right or a duty), it is not difficult to imagine a decision that might produce the greatest overall happiness but may be associated with a less than desirable circumstance, such as moving a family from their home to build a freeway or constructing a large building that deprives a smaller neighbour of solar access. Such examples illustrate how controversial utilitarianism can be in some situations.

Intergenerational equity

A problem for all approaches to sustainability ethics concerns the issue of intergenerational equity inherent in almost every definition of sustainable development and sustainable design. This problem is known after Parfit (1984) as the *non-identity problem* and comes about like this. We can appreciate that all manner of design-type decisions will affect social arrangements, the way people conduct their lives, and ultimately the duration of people's lives. Since these factors will influence the choice of reproduction partners and the timing of reproduction, the decisions ultimately determine that one group of people, and not another, will exist in the future. When we take into account our decisions and the decisions of all other architects and policy makers this obviously raises certain problems – 'exactly what *future generation* are we dealing with?' and 'how can we be held responsible by a later generation for a decision when, albeit for the decision, they would not have existed at all?' 'How can we have a duty to a future generation (and presume to know anything of their needs) when we don't know the composition of the generation?'

Traditional moral thinking usually concerns same-people choices, yet moral thinking about future generations usually concerns possible different-people choices. How in such cases can we make the best decisions? Parfit (1984) provides one illustration of the non-identity problem with a type of decision that needs to be made in the design of a sustainable building: should we allow a natural resource to be depleted or should we encourage its conservation? He gives the following example. Under an action of allowing the depletion of natural resources the quality of life would be slightly better for everyone for 300 years than under a policy of conservation. Thereafter, however, it would be considerably worse. Parfit considers that after 300 years of the policy of depletion an entirely different population will exist than would have existed if conservation had been the policy. Hence depletion benefits those who live for the first 300 years and is worse for no one who is born later (since without the policy these people would not have existed at all). Depletion is therefore worse for no one, but conservation is worse for those who live in the first 300 years. If we imagine that for either depletion or conservation the same number of people would live, then depletion is wrong if those who live are worse off, or have a lower quality of life. In the case where different numbers of people might exist then the decision on which action to adopt becomes even more difficult; then we must deal with quality/quantity trade-offs. Since many design decisions might affect future generations in this way, if Parfit is right, then it would seem that many actions taken to provide a better future in fact benefited no one. Parfit suggests intuitively that depletion is not the favoured option, but fails to find a unified theory that satisfactorily explains why this is the case. If we assume that 'existing' is a benefit then a total view utilitarian approach defined in impersonal terms comes close to providing an answer. With this approach when a range of alternative decisions is open to us now, we ought to choose those actions that on the whole would most likely lead to the best consequences. Leaving aside questions of determining exactly what we mean by the 'best consequences' and the uncertainty of future predictions, when considered from a person-affecting viewpoint even this approach gives rise to certain problems. Can a loss in quality of life of a future generation, (or the total quantity of happiness, or whatever makes life worthwhile) be balanced (or even outweighed) by increases in population? Can an increase in the quality of life of many outweigh a small number who would have a quality of life that is overall just worth living?

Where do these arguments leave us in making our day-to-day decisions? If our decisions could be reasonably anticipated to cause changes to living conditions so that at least some people in future generations, no matter who they are, would be worse off or that they would live in unfavourable conditions, then intuitively it would seem that we cannot pretend that we have no duties to them. Some argue that we have these duties to future generations because we are bound to future individuals as a transgenerational community. Partridge (1981) suggests that a 'self transcending concern' for communities and the institutions that define our culture to flourish beyond one's lifespan is a psychological motivation for a concern for the future. Adams (1997), on the other hand, suggests that the foundations of an ethical theory regarding future generations flows from a commitment to the future of humanity as a vast project of interrelated and overlapping projects shared by the human race as a whole.

While again we might feel intuitively that this is correct, we are still left with several sticky issues regarding design for sustainability. Since we cannot be sure of the needs and preferences of future generations (the near future and especially the distant future) our best attempts now at sustainable designs might be overturned in the future. Needs and preferences in a market-driven world can be manufactured by advertising campaigns. Buildings originally designed in the 1970s to operate on passive solar principles without air conditioning now have air conditioning installed, not because they didn't operate effectively, but because the preferences of the occupants have changed. A second but related issue concerns the rights of future generations to seek a quality of life higher than ours. We would probably not disagree with the aspiration of a future better society, as Adams suggests, 'more just, more rewarding and more peaceful', but measuring quality of life, for example, in terms of bigger houses or more appliances is another matter.

These approaches to ethics raise issues of interest and concern, and while putting our decision-making into a broad context they do not explicitly address how in practice we might tackle making sustainable architecture. The problem is that most of these ethical traditions developed when philosophers worried mainly about how human beings related to each other, rather than issues of the environment and issues of sustainability, as we are familiar with them today. To help position such issues in our decision-making we need to turn to the relatively recent branch of philosophy, known as environmental ethics, that attempts to frame the moral relations between human beings and their natural environment.

Environmental ethics

Environmental ethics attempts to explain how human behaviour toward the natural world can and/or should be governed by moral norms.

In the 1970s the Norwegian philosopher Arne Naess argued that Western philosophy is founded on an outdated view of the world, in which human beings are understood as separate from one another and from the natural world. He suggested that recent work in physics and ecology does not support such an understanding of the world. The 'new sciences' recognize humans not as isolated, separate objects but rather as having interconnected relationships with each other and constantly changing relationships with everything around them – part of the flow of energy, the web of life. In analysing the environmental movement of the time he identified two key strands; one he termed shallow and the other deep (see Naess 1989). The shallow movement was primarily concerned with human welfare and how issues such as the exhaustion of natural resources may affect this welfare. In contrast, the deep environmental movement was concerned with fundamental philosophical questions about the ways in which humans relate to their environment. In particular, deep ecology incorporated insights from modern physics and ecology into human understanding of the natural world. From this perspective, the first priority in analysing environmental issues must be in transforming one's fundamental way of looking at the world, to develop what Naess calls a more 'holistic' outlook. Although most environmental ethic discussions focus on the natural environment, King (2000) argues that this view must be extended to include the built environment so that we can better understand the 'making and contrivance' of the places that most of us inhabit.

To link sustainability to the moral class in operational terms we shall adopt Sylvan and Bennett's (1994) three broad categories of shallow, intermediate and deep views of environmental ethics, locating the intermediate position between Naess's labels of shallow and deep.

Shallow environmentalism and the precautionary principle

> *Shallow Environmentalism* is anthropocentric. Few constraints are imposed upon the treatment of the environment providing that its treatment does not interfere with the interests of other humans. By contrast, however, with non-environmental ethics it does take a long-term view of environmental issues, and it does consider future human generations. For these reasons it is often described as resource management or husbandry.
>
> (Sylvan and Bennett 1994: 63)

As we have seen, the term sustainable development is most commonly defined in anthropocentric terms, with no inherent value assigned to ecological systems outside the instrumental value they have to humans. Shallow environmentalism has some echoes with the rights/duty-based approach to moral behaviour, the difference being that rights can never be taken as absolute. The 1992 *Rio Declaration on Environment and Development* fits within this anthropocentric view and is framed essentially in terms of long-term resource management for the benefit of humans. Its Principle 1 states that: 'Human beings are at the centre of concerns for sustainable development. They are entitled to a healthy and productive life in harmony with nature.' Principle 4 follows with: 'In order to achieve sustainable development environmental protection shall constitute an integral part of the development process.' This rather contradictory combination of sustainability and development is regarded by Bengs as an oxymoron:[10]

> Sustainability indicates caretaking and maintenance, the repetition of certain procedures. In this respect sustainability implies a circular notion of time. Development on the other hand is in our culture connected to a continuous accumulation of capital, material, services, knowledge and anything that is commodified. Accordingly, development implies a linear notion of time. Is it possible to integrate those two comprehensions of time into one concept? Can a circle be a straight line? . . .
> Maybe sustainable in this context does not mean unchanged stability but continuous development, taking into account the potential repercussions of nature? Then the prime care is that of accumulation, not of nature. Nature can be menaced as long as severe backlashes to development are avoided. In case of nature's backlash, the surplus of the society is supposedly allocated to protect nature. The fundamental matter giving rise to the environmental crises, i.e. accumulation, is seen as the solution of this very matter as well: accumulation is the secret of sustainability. Sustainable development is to fit into an entirely linear concept of time. . . . The sustainability of development has to be guaranteed – nature is a part of the action programme.
>
> (Bengs 1993: 21–2)

Although in this view nature is a resource to be used, the *precautionary principle* applies: decisions should always err on the side of caution where ecological assets are at risk. Under the precautionary principle, if there is any doubt about the long-term repercussions of an action on human welfare, then the only moral action is to play safe, including preserving the components of our existing environment so as not to deprive future generations of a possible good.[11]

This idea of acting according to the *precautionary principle* has no place in an empirical (technocratic) view of the world because it is only invoked when knowledge is absent. When one operates in a world of 'logically derived facts' the need for such speculation is eliminated by risk management analysis. Events are assigned a probability and a course of action is chosen impartially from a number of alternatives, according to the estimated minimum undesirable effects of the human interventions or the likely maximum net benefits. It brings with it a view that if a future predicament is foreseen, then appropriate technologies will be invented that will cope with the problem, providing that analysis shows it is the best way to expend scarce capital and resources now. Industries will invest research and development funds when the incentives of monetary returns are sufficient. Similarly if an unforeseen predicament arises in the future, technologies will be invented to deal with the problem, providing this is considered at the time to be the most appropriate course of action.

Intermediate environmentalism

The next group of positions take a less instrumental view.

> *Intermediate positions* can be distinguished as rejecting the notion that humans and human projects are the sole items of value; however serious human concerns always come first [have greater value]. These positions acknowledge the value-in-their-own-right of some at least of animals, eco-systems, forests, and other parts of the environment as a whole in addition to their value for human purposes.
>
> (Sylvan and Bennett 1994: 63)

Much of the environmental conservation movement takes at least an interme-diate position: we should protect wilderness, whales and birds *both* for our own good *and* for their own sakes. And why only consider human and non-human animals? Once the ambit of those who are to be regarded as stakeholders in decisions extends beyond humans, it is difficult to establish a cut-off point. A 'life-centred' ethic requires that in deciding how to act we should consider the impact of the action on every living thing, including plants and other organ-isms. An 'everything' ethic takes inanimate as well as animate objects into account – rights for rocks, as Elliott puts it (Elliot 1991: 288).[12] This is not as outlandish as it may at first seem. We can find ourselves feeling that it is somehow morally better to build with minimal impact on the physical soil and rocks of ground form – touching the earth lightly in a physical sense – rather than gouging out excavations into that land. In Australia, two of the most hard-fought and famous battles over environmental issues have been about inanimate 'objects', both in the mountainous island state of Tasmania. The first was the loss of the beautiful Lake Pedder under a much larger dammed lake through the construction of a hydroelectric scheme (the environmentalists lost), the second was the loss of the 'free-running' Gordon River under a proposed second hydro-electric scheme (the environmentalists won). Although the value of these places could be framed in terms of ecosystems and human perceptions of beauty, the rhetoric of the environmentalists emphasized their intrinsic 'right' to continue existence as water-and-rock elements.

Often both shallow and deep environmental positions lead to the same action: conservation and preservation of nature, and care over our use of the environment. They do, though, indicate a fundamentally different attitude towards the environment, well illustrated by the issue of natural wilderness areas. In shallow environmentalism, natural wilderness is highly valued as a place for humans to experience and enjoy. Debate centres on the competing attractions of the maintenance of this experience for future generations and the benefits to our own and future generations of mining, water collection or other activities in the wilderness area. The degree to which access (constructing a road through a wilderness area or constructing an 'eco-lodge' to house visitors) might degrade the experience while making it available to more people is also important. In this debate, the relative values (typically visual interest and biodiversity) of the area compared to others are deemed to be relevant. The balance of trade-offs has human interests on both sides of the balance.

In intermediate environmentalism, natural wilderness as an ecosystem has intrinsic value, and inaccessible wilderness (with neither roads nor lodges) is highly valued because it allows other species to exist without human interference. The balance of trade-offs does not have human interests on both sides – although it is still humans making the judgements, and the weights may favour human interests.

Deep environmentalism

In 'deep positions' humanity is pushed firmly back into the status of one amongst many components of the environment.

> *Deep positions* are characterised by the rejection of the notion that humans and human projects are the sole items of value, and further by the rejection of the notion that humans and human projects are always more valuable than all other things in the world.
>
> (Sylvan and Bennett 1994: 63)

In deep positions, humans are not held to have a privileged status in the environment. Both the 'Sole Value Assumption' and the 'Greater Value Assumption' are rejected (Sylvan and Bennett 1994: 90). It follows that humans have no more right to occupy a site with their building than any other potential uses of the site that are incompatible with this human use. Humans are placed in the same position as a lion or tiger that might dominate their site because of their physical and mental capabilities but have no moral right to that dominating position. Moreover, the *unique* ability of humans to recognize that they are dominating means that they have an ethical responsibility to allow other species space to live; one assumes that lions never claim to see things from an antelope's point of view.

Another way of framing a deep approach is to regard not individuals but species, populations and ecological systems as subjects of concern. In this framing of ecological holism, it is the biosphere as a whole and the major ecosystems that constitute the biosphere (rainforest systems and wetlands systems, for example) that should always be the centre of our concerns. James Lovelock uses the ancient Greek word 'Gaia' for the Earth as a single living entity 'in which the Earth's living matter, air, oceans, and land surface form a complex system which can be seen as a single organism and which has the capacity to keep our planet a fit place for life' (Lovelock 1987: x). What happens to individuals, or even species, is unimportant relative to the *health* of these major systems as a whole. Insofar as a healthy biotic community is considered to be one that has the biological capacity for self-renewal and its degeneration is the loss of this capacity, we are left with several unresolved issues. First, how do we view the impact on individuals within a system that may be harmed by our actions even though the system as a whole continues? And second, since all biotic systems undergo gradual evolution, how can we define *health* at a point in time? Climate change, for example, may result in some systems degenerating while others are enhanced.

'Taking into account' does not necessarily imply equal weighting on the significance of the impact on different individuals or subsystems. If we do give inter-species rights the same importance as intra-species (human) rights, then it seems to follow that ecological development should be a minimal intervention to allow humans to survive at about the same quality of living as other species. If we attribute to plants and rocks equal rather than minor consideration, then we are even more constrained. Further, since many of these positions are associated with an advocacy of a gradual but drastic reduction in human population, we would be managing a process of drastic reduction in requirements for buildings and settlements.[13] Although one can follow this argument and recognize its moral position, very few humans seem prepared to live by this ethic. We might intellectualize that we are the problem, but we may well still seek to ameliorate the problem rather than eliminate the privileged position of humans.

Though deep environmentalism has taken many twists and turns since the early 1970s, this plea for a profound change in the way we Westerners think about the world is still at its heart. Not surprisingly, deep environmentalists argue that such a change in world view entails a corresponding change in what we consider as valuable, leading ultimately to a change of environmental ethics. One surprisingly different approach to thinking about environmental issues has been proposed by Warwick Fox, in his book *Toward a Transpersonal Ecology*. He suggests a change in the metaphysics such that a conception of self not as 'narrow, atomistic and particle-like' but rather 'wide, expansive and field-like' renders superfluous the traditional approach to ethics conceived as duties towards others (Fox 1991: 217). He argues that if we accept the transpersonal ecology view of self – that we extend into the world around us – then our actions in the world are really actions toward ourselves and we will therefore instinctively protect the (natural) world around us.

If we analyse a proposal to construct a building that we would consider resource intensive from this point of view, then a very different picture emerges compared with other positions we have considered. Such a proposal is a violation of ourselves; a cause of grief and suffering. Harm to the world around us (our family, friends, animals, buildings, the region in which we live) is harm to ourselves; protection of the world around us is self-defence. The personal nature of this offence might then lead us to campaign against such a building being constructed. Similarly the destruction of virgin rainforest even in a faraway country to provide timber for building, or the insertion of a large and ugly multinational chain's hotel in the delicate fabric of a Pacific island village, are no less violations of ourselves which we should mourn.

Even this brief summary is sufficient to indicate that deep environmentalism offers a very different way of analysing environmental issues, and thus a different approach to environmental ethics, than the more traditional approaches previously outlined. But while environmental ethics gives us an insight into possible moral relationships between humans and the non-human world, it says nothing about procedures that might in a practical way inform real-world responsible decision-making.

Discourse ethics

Although we may not be able to agree on the theoretical aspects of moral principles, designing for sustainability in the real world requires that human stakeholders reach some consensus on the moral aspects of practical issues. Discourse ethics, which owes its foundations to Jürgen Habermas (1990), offers a process to tackle this problem. As Habermas explains, the key to discourse ethics is the communication that takes place between the participants in the process.

> Discourses take place in particular social contexts and are subject to the limitations of time and space. Their participants are not Kant's intelligible characters but real human beings driven by motives in addition to the one permitted motive of the search for truth.
>
> (Habermas 1990: 92)

The ethical quality of discourse ethics stems from the mutual recognition and acceptance of the others who participate in the process.[14] Discourse ethics is able to account for the full complexity of real-world decision-making situations because the reasoned arguments that participants bring to the table are inseparable from the social, cultural, economic and knowledge bases that informs their contributions. Decisions made as a result of structured discursive reasoning are in every way as rational as socio-technologically based instrumental reasoning. Because the aim of the discourse is to ensure that all suppositions are transparent, differing views may be projected; a utilitarianist's contribution on social and public good or a deep environmetalist's view on intrinsic value. Sabine O'Hara explains how discourse ethics may contribute to sustainability:

1) Discursive ethics adds a contextual dimension to the universal principle of a morality based on human reason. This dimension makes connections between human–human and human–environmental systems implicit and thus questions assumptions of isolated, self-interest motivated agency.
2) Discursive ethics adds a communal dimension to the expression of human reason which cannot be expressed in isolation . . . Socio-ecological complexities of sustainability cannot be adequately addressed in disciplinary isolation but rather require broad-based interdisciplinary discourse.
3) Discursive ethics cannot be conceived as a purely theoretical thought exercise and therefore adds a practical dimension to moral decision making which links private and public spheres.

(O'Hara 1998)

Imagine three people holding shallow, intermediate and deep environmentalist positions meeting to discuss a proposed new building in a sensitive area. A successful discourse about the issue will depend on two things: the individual's inalienable right to say yes or no to the others' validity claims, and of them overcoming their egocentric viewpoint. In other words, each participant must respect the rights and dignity of the others. What we are likely to find in the discourse is that after hearing the different views, discussion will quickly focus on the impacts of alternatives, including the impacts of not building. Some options are likely to be rejected by all three people, narrowing the field. Others may be found not to have a credible argument that can be constructed in their support. What is left are proposals that while they may not be favoured by all three people, are the 'least disfavoured' by their non-supporters. This does not necessarily solve the problem, but through such discourse possibilities emerge that none of the participants originally entertained. In this instance our three participants could be advocates for the full range of entities due moral consideration, for example, the deep environmentalist could talk for the trees, and each in their way may speak for future generations, but none of them could truly be said to represent all entities. Participants may in a real sense represent a human constituency by passing on their views or even casing votes on their behalf, but they cannot in the same way represent nature. The importance of stakeholder representation in decision-making is discussed in the next chapter, and we shall return to notions of discourse and the endeavour to find cohesion in Chapter 7.

Beautiful acts

There is a (probably apocryphal) story of a Hollywood film producer who at the end of a heated argument with his studio's boss thundered: 'Well, if you don't like my principles . . . I have others'. These various ethical positions are not a menu from which we can pick to suit our circumstances. On the other hand, we have to recognize a plurality of positions amongst different cultures, religions and individuals. People holding these different positions will 'see' the problems and issues of a sustainable architecture differently. In coming to agreement, we engage in discourse that seeks to comprehend the impacts of options as seen from this multiplicity of positions. In doing this we must also acknowledge that the condition of manufactured risk demands that we deal positively with the issue of uncertainty that Bauman sets out as the main requirement for a future ethics:

> Ethics . . . must deal with what-has-not-happened-yet, with a future that is endemically the realm of uncertainty and the playfield of conflicting scenarios. Visualization can never pretend to offer the kind of certainty which experts with their scientific knowledge and with greater or lesser credibility claim to offer. The duty to visualize the future impact of action (undertaken or not undertaken) means acting under the pressure of acute uncertainty. The moral stance consists precisely in seeing to it that this uncertainty is neither dismissed nor suppressed, but consciously embraced.
>
> (Bauman 1993: 221)

In considering ethical approaches to understanding sustainable architecture we should ask the question posed by Foucault (1997): 'how did it come about that all of Western culture began to revolve around the obligation of truth which has taken a lot of different forms?' It may in the end be impossible to prove the *truth* of any ethical view. The clue to the solution may in fact derive from the nature of architecture and of architects themselves. This can be illustrated by borrowing from Naess's ethical approach to environmental affairs that follows his interpretation of Kant's metaphysics of morals. This approach has more in common with Aristotle's 'activity in accordance with complete virtue' than other traditional approaches to ethics.

For Naess 'moral acts are acts motivated by the intention to follow a moral law or a code of behaviour, that is, we do our moral duty solely out of respect for that duty' (Naess 1986). This approach can lead to extensive moralizing about showing more responsibility, more concern and better morals. Certainly at times we need to be made aware of our ethical shortcomings, but each of us will more easily be changed through encouragement and through a deeper perception of our own self and what constitutes total good design. If then we do something that we should do not according to a moral law, but out of inclination and with pleasure (and not for selfish motives), then we perform a *beautiful* act.

A sustainable architecture will follow if we encourage architects towards *beautiful* acts as a virtue, working on their inclinations rather than a prescription of duty. But neither can this virtue become simply a habit of good actions acquired by practice. As Kant himself explains:

> For unless this aptitude results from considered, firm, and continually puri-fied principles, then, like any other mechanism of technically practical reason, it is neither armed for all situations nor adequately secured against the changes the new temptations could bring about.
>
> (Kant 1996: 148)

What this means is that rather than prescribe a limited range of sustainable building solutions we should support an increased richness and diversity of solutions crafted in care and joy. The requisite care flows naturally when we feel and conceive sustainable architecture as a protection of ourselves. The joy stems from the knowledge that we are contributing to something bigger than ourselves, and something that will be worthy of enduring well past our time. This is a goal to which we can all contribute individually, both at a local level and a global level. But how might such beautiful acts be brought about?

In the next chapter we shall discuss how architects as decision-makers act with and for other stakeholders in a design and development process, and how a sustainable architecture is advanced (or hindered) by design advice and regu-lations that attempt to influence or control the ends and means of design.

Notes

1 Bauman (1993: 11) asserts that:

> Moral phenomena are inherently 'non-rational' . . . Ethics is thought of after the pattern of Law. As Law does, it strives to define the 'proper' and the 'improper'

actions in situations on which it takes a stand. It sets for itself an ideal (rarely if ever reached in practice) of churning up exhaustive and unambiguous definitions; such as would provide clear-cut rules for the choice between proper and improper and leave no 'grey area' of ambivalence and multiple interpretations. In other words, it acts on the assumption that in each life-situation one choice can and should be decreed to be good in opposition to numerous bad ones, and so acting in all situations can be rational while the actors are, as they should be, rational as well.

2 It is perhaps surprising that little has been written explicitly on the subject of ethics and sustainability, and even less has been written on the subject dealing with built environment issues. Warwick Fox (2000: 2) describes the failure of environmental ethics to embrace issues of the constructed environment as a 'blind spot'.

3 As Baier (1969: 53) states, ' . . . every normative statement requires some appraisal as its backing, and value assessments can and typically do function in this way.'

4 For example, John Foster in his introduction to a collection of papers entitled *Value Nature?* asks the questions

> How do we, and how should we, express our sense of the worth and practical importance of our natural environment, and the significance of our relations with other living things? How do we include such values within the processes of social decision-making?
>
> (Foster 1997: 1)

5 Baier (1969: 50)

> It would undoubtedly be best if the qualifying expression 'intrinsic value' could be altogether banned from the literature. It has caused more trouble than any other technical term and has not, to my way of thinking, advanced our comprehension of value one bit.

6 In his essay *The Historical Roots of Our Ecological Crisis*, Lynn White Jr (1967) argues that, because in the Judaeo-Christian tradition humans were given *rightful* domination over nature, at least in Western Christian manifestations of this tradition, humans have exploited the earth's resources for selfish reasons and without regard to the consequences.

7 'Candidates for moral standing include animals, plants, species, natural objects like mountains, rivers, and wilderness areas, and even the earth itself' (Des Jardins 2001: 103).

8 The general elements of this table are based on a presentation given by Warwick Fox to The Ethics and Building Conference, The University of Central Lancashire, April, 1999.

9 *The Universal Declaration of Human Rights* was adopted by the United Nations in 1948. Article 25 states

> Everyone has the right to a standard of living adequate for the health and well-being of himself and of his family, including food, clothing, housing and medical care and necessary social services, and the right to security in the event of unemployment, sickness, disability, widowhood, old age or other lack of livelihood in circumstances beyond his control.

10 Daly (1993: 267–8) dismisses the idea of 'sustainable growth' succinctly in his Impossibility Theorem:

Impossibility theorems are the very foundation of science. . . . By respecting impossibility theorems we avoid wasting resources on projects that are bound to fail. Therefore economists should be very interested . . . that it is impossible for the world economy to grow its way out of poverty and environmental degradation. In other words, sustainable growth is impossible. . . . The term 'sustainable growth' when applied to the economy is a bad oxymoron – self-contradictory as prose and unevocative as poetry. . . . When something grows it gets bigger. When something develops it gets different. . . . The term 'sustainable development' therefore makes sense for the economy but only if understood as 'development without growth'. . . . Politically it is very difficult to admit that growth, with its almost religious connotations of ultimate goodness, must be limited. . . . To delude ourselves into believing that growth is still possible and desirable if only we label it 'sustainable' or colour it 'green' will just delay the inevitable transition and make it more painful.

11 This can have radical implications: Peter Fawcett argues that 'An architect especially should be expected to see clearly that each CBD skyscraper may be a theft from the future; and that each domestic air-conditioner specified today is a nail in tomorrow's coffin' (Fawcett 1998: 68). But the precautionary principle does not always lead to the best possible outcomes. Anthony Giddens (1999a) explained in his Reith Lecture on the subject of risk:

The notion of the precautionary principle first emerged in Germany about 15 years ago, in the context of the ecological debates that were carried on there. At its simplest, it proposes that action on environmental issues (and by inference other forms of risk) should be taken even though there is insecure scientific evidence about them. . . . Yet the precautionary principle isn't always helpful or even applicable as a means of coping with problems of risk and responsibility. The precept of 'staying close to nature', or of limiting innovation rather than embracing it, can't always apply. The reason is that the balance of benefits and dangers from scientific and technological advance, and other forms of social change too, is imponderable. We may need quite often to be bold rather than cautious in supporting scientific innovation or other forms of change. After all, one root of the term risk in the original Portuguese means 'to dare' . . . there can be no question of merely taking a negative attitude towards risk. Risk always needs to be disciplined, but active risk-taking is a core element of a dynamic economy and an innovative society.

(Giddens 1999a)

12 These possible objects of 'moral considerability' are passive subjects in the terminology of decision-making that we shall describe in Chapter 4.
13 The process of caring for human cultural heritage with a much-reduced human population would itself be problematic.
14 Such a proposal is not without its critics. Foucault (1997: 298) says

I am quite interested in his [Habermas] work, although I know he completely disagrees with my views. While I, for my part, tend to be a little more in agreement with what he says, I have always had a problem insofar as he gives communicative relations this place which is so important and above all, a function that I would call 'utopian.' The idea that there could exist a state of communication that would allow games of truth to circulate freely, without any constraints or coercive effects, seems utopian to me.

4 Objectives

4.1 Stakeholders in urban sustainability: The Hanoi 'old town' in 2002, with its character of narrow fronted deep 'tube houses', street-edge commerce, and traffic where motor-cycles are replacing bicycles (photographer Pham Khanh Toan).

The discussion of ethics in Chapter 3 leads us to ask of sustainable architecture: sustainable in terms of what stakeholder's continued existence or present and future well-being? This is rarely explicit in the plethora of published advice and regulations that aim to assist or regulate design. In this chapter we shall frame sustainability as an objective of stakeholders, frame architects as active stakeholders who (along with others) make decisions about the best means to achieve those outcomes, and consider how design advice (including books, journals, and regulations) seeks to guide or direct the range of possible decisions. In particular, we shall highlight the very different nature of the kinds of books and regulations that refer to the means of achieving sustainability-related objectives (advocating or requiring particular building forms and materials), and those that refer to the performance of designs (for example, advocating or requiring particular levels of energy use, carbon dioxide (CO_2) emissions, or materials durability).

Stakeholders[1]

Imagine a client organization that asks its architect to prepare a highly detailed brief for a building, with *all* of the aims and requirements for the project set out, so that all will be clear when decisions come to be made. When it is delivered, the client finds that only about a fifth refers to its own appreciation of its needs. Why all this other stuff? It asks. That's the brief for the other stakeholders' objectives, is the reply: the regulators, the neighbours, the community, us as architects, the other design professionals, and the planet. One of the aspects of performing a beautiful act is to account in the design for all the stakeholders.

From the discussion in Chapter 3, it was shown how the stakeholders in any design process will be some subset of the moral class. The inclusion or exclusion of present and future generations of people, creatures, inanimate objects and systems will depend on our values and ethical standpoints, and we might regard the earth as a whole to be a passive stakeholder in all or some of our decisions if we frame the earth as a whole as a member of the moral class. *Passive* stakeholders are those on whose behalf decisions are made by architects and others, but who (or which, in the case of inanimate stakeholders) have no active part in the decision making themselves. *Active* stakeholders include all decision-makers, no matter how minor, and no matter whether the deciding is directed to a particular building or to a whole class of buildings, as occurs in the preparation of building regulations. Investors, occupants, regulators, builders, professional designers (architects, engineers) and their clients are all potentially active stakeholders to the extent that they have a say in decisions for a particular project.

Stakeholders have (or have attributed to them) explicit or implicit objectives, from general and somewhat vague aims such as happiness and sustainability itself, to specifics such as reduced ozone depletion potential. Objectives drive the design process, and an expansion of the objectives consciously taken into account to encompass the objectives of sustainability is fundamental to any attempt to promote more sustainable architecture. Objectives are frequently closely interconnected, and conflict between objectives is common. Means of achieving objectives of long life, low cost and architecturally fashionable, for example, may conflict. Dealing with these conflicts and contradictions requires the explicit or implicit assumption of priorities, which is in turn largely determined by our view of the relative seriousness of the consequences of failure or shortfall.

Achieving the overall objective of sustainable architecture involves steps of determining the animate and inanimate stakeholders, identifying their objectives for sustainability (and, of course, their other objectives), and finding (designing) means of achieving performances that meet them. Only a few of these performances will be measurable in any quantifiable way. Of those that are, many will be expressed in terms of acceptable limits; if the design promises performances within those limits it is acceptable, otherwise not. Before we look at the nature of the advice available to us on these performances and means to achieve them, we need to digress briefly into design and decision processes and the nature of design knowledge.

Design and decision processes

The discussion so far may appear to suggest that decisions are always the result of carefully considered assessments and balancing of stakeholders' objectives and the available means to achieve those objectives. Even where the architect and all other stakeholders are involved in a discursive practice, as discussed in Chapter 3, this is unlikely to happen. In practice an architect must make many decisions quickly and simply, on the basis of apparent fittingness with the right thing to do rather than deep analysis (Beach 1990: xiii).[2] Designers are also typically concerned with many decisions at the same time, switching from one to another in an attempt to find a fit between them, and initially regard most decisions as provisional anyway. Moreover, design problems are notoriously difficult to manage, to the extent of being labelled wicked:

> A class of social system problems which are ill-formulated, where the information is confusing, where there are many clients and decision makers with conflicting values, and where the ramifications in the whole system are thoroughly confusing.
>
> (Horst Rittel, quoted in Buchanan 1992: 15)

One of the distinguishing features of wicked problems is that their subject matter is potentially universal in scope. Some strategy for making the problem manageable is imperative. Designers draw on their store of images to identify or recognize key features of a new situation to determine what portion of their knowledge is likely to be pertinent to it. Skilful practitioners learn to conduct frame experiments in which they impose a kind of coherence on messy situations and thereby discover consequences and implications of their chosen frames. Long webs of 'what if I try this?' speculations are spun out in the process of making a design. In this way designers come to understand the possibilities and scope of a problem through a circle of making proposals and reflecting on their implications. From time to time, their efforts to give order to a situation provoke unexpected outcomes – 'back talk' that gives the situation a new meaning. They listen and reframe the problem. It is this ensemble of problem framing, on-the-spot experiment, detection of consequences and implications, back talk and response to back talk, that constitutes a reflective conversation with the materials of a situation – the artistry of professional practice (see Schön 1987: 157–8).[3]

New situations rarely exactly match past situations, or the predefined problems and answers set out in prescriptive design advice (we discuss this further below). Rather, the design enterprise itself involves research, triggered by questions to be answered in the design situation and with the research results immediately pressed into action in design decisions (Schön 1987: 308–9). The research may be as apparently straightforward as the 'simple sequential examination of the place in order to understand it . . . as an interacting system' that McHarg advocates (McHarg 1969: 151) as a part of designing with nature. It may also investigate materials, patterns of use, or any other facet of design. Results are not always as expected, and decision-making proceeds by fits and starts. Beach comments:

> Opportunities (plans) beget goals. Goals are modified as plans are refined. Principles that at first seem irrelevant turn out to be relevant, often painfully so. Plans that at first seem straightforward turn out to be impossible to implement or to fall short of achieving their goal. Goals that look desirable become less so when the requirements for their achievement become clear.
>
> (Beach 1990: 15)

Knowledge

The imprecision and uncertainty surrounding sustainability and the means for its achievement make knowledge, how it is used, and how relevance and ignorance are dealt with, all particularly important.

Architects embark on a design project, 'with a store of knowledge about what has lead up to it, what is going on and why, and what his or her role is to be in the proceedings' (Beach 1990: 51) and use this as a trigger and starting point for case-specific research. During the design process they draw on what Downing (1992a) calls an image bank: a repository of stored images of buildings, places, events and experiences, including their own past work. Architects probe their memories for portions of their knowledge with similar features in order to recognize or identify aspects of the new situation. A portion of their knowledge will involve images of what they believe to be true regarding the environmental and other aspects of sustainability in design. These images of 'what is' are derived from the architects' experiences of, and ideas about, environmental issues, building, stakeholders and their objectives, the role of the architect and the nature of design – as with the three diverse images of sustainability (natural, cultural and technical) that we discussed in Chapter 2. These images will be important influences on how the architects frame the contexts of the new project. In turn, this framing will influence what actions and outcomes are considered possible, necessary or appropriate. Contexts change over time and during the design process. As the contexts change, frames need to be updated accordingly (Beach 1990: 53). The dynamic, sense-making nature of this process has been represented in terms of story-making in relation to decision-making (Beach 1990) and, in relation to design, of reflective conversation (Schön 1987) and argument (Buchanan 1992; Arnheim 1993).

Beach maintains that:

> The knowledge (image constituents) that constitutes a frame is largely represented in the form of stories, however fragmentary, and that it is this quality that gives continuity and meaning to the events that occur in that frame.
> (Beach 1990: 22)

The designers' knowledge of the conventions of stories (plots, contexts, aims, characters, etc.) and generic knowledge of similar situations (for example, the design of a house) allows them to deal with scant information initially and to assess what other material is needed to give 'the story' completeness, continuity and plausibility (Pennington and Hastie 1988). Thus an architect will have an image of the story of the design project he or she is about to undertake. This image enables an appreciation of the various aspects of the project and suggests where there may be gaps in the story and where he or she is likely to have to draw on design advice to clarify issues. Most importantly, it provides a frame within which the architect can project into the future and imagine what could be. Forecasting the future usually consists of extrapolating the past and present to construct a plausible story about the future in which the architect is an active participant – a pretend-like, active, version of the story that constitutes the frame of the context (Beach 1990: 38).[4]

Relevance and ignorance

Connections between objectives and means in this projection to the future are made with the tools of knowledge. In defining problems, we apply (when relevant) science, other systematic approaches and forms of knowing, creativity and intuition. Whether or not it is explicit and systematic, in any contested field like sustainable architecture questions about the nature and legitimacy of knowledge arise.[5] Michael Smithson (1988), in his book *Ignorance and Uncertainty*, has developed an instructive way to help us relate relevance to a design problem and to the purposefulness of designers, occupants, and other stakeholders. He begins by drawing attention to the importance of point of view and proposes a working definition of ignorance as 'A is ignorant from B's point of view if A fails to agree with or show awareness of ideas which B defines as actually or potentially valid' (Smithson 1988: 6). If we could stand outside of our own decision-making, we might then ask ourselves questions about four types of ignorance:

1   Absence: Is the relevant knowledge present (and sufficiently emphasized)?
2   Confusion: Is there a distortion in definition of the kind of knowledge, resulting in a definition that is not fully relevant to the problem?

3 Uncertainty: Is the knowledge uncertain, and what degree of certainty is relevant?
4 Inaccuracy: How accurate does the knowledge need to be?

Absence appears to be a straightforward concept. For example, until recently contributions to greenhouse gas emissions have generally been absent from consideration in building design problems, as the decision-makers have not thought it to be relevant for them to take greenhouse gases into account. Someone bringing to mind a 'technology image' of sustainability is likely to lament the absence of knowledge of someone with a 'cultural image' in mind, and vice versa. Solutions to the design problem *as understood by* A will be irrelevant to the design problem *as understood by* B if their perceptions of the relevancy of knowledge do not intersect.

Confusion in defining relevant objectives or means arises when knowledge is defined in a way that is a distortion of how it should be defined in order to address the particular problem. We shall show in Chapter 6 how the objective of low greenhouse gas emissions has been widely confused with the objective of low energy use, so that regulations and advice intended to promote the former objective have instead addressed the latter and missed important aspects of the problem. Like absence, assertions of confusion depend on points of view. Good problem definition is more likely where the 'experts' share both images and knowledge with other stakeholders (including each other), so that both the objectives and means evolve by inquiry rather than being taken for granted.

Uncertainty and inaccuracy can relate to both ends and means. They occur when there is a need to make assumptions about the future, and/or there are limitations inherent in the quantification of data. As uncertainty is a fundamental feature of nearly all sustainability issues, our discussions about the natural and cultural environments, our information about building materials, about costs, and about people's ends must be seen in this light. This is particularly important when dealing with design advice. While the advice-givers may have at least some appreciation of the potential for error, this is not always assiduously communicated to those who receive the advice. Without appropriate caveats, users interpret the guidance as giving accurate and certain information when this is likely not to be the case. Some aspects of uncertainty can be treated probabilistically, with statistical techniques. For example, estimates of climate change, based on attempts to predict the long-term future state of the coupled non-linear chaotic climate system, are based entirely on probability estimates of subsystem states.

For any particular design problem, uncertainty may or may not be important. Consider the collection of rainwater off the roof of a building. If the water is for drinking or fire fighting, and this is the only supply, then a mistake would have severe consequences. In this case dealing with the uncertainty and variability of the rain would mean that a large factor of safety is designed into the solution. In the case where a mistake would matter less, where the rainwater is collected for the occasional watering of pot plants, then dealing with the uncertainty can be less onerous.

Compared with uncertainty, inaccuracy is a fairly straightforward concept. Scientific instruments for measuring and recording physical effects (for example, heat flows, temperatures and energy use) in the objective world have greatly improved the accuracy of available knowledge about the performance of buildings. Computer simulations provide sophisticated modelling tools that can predict, with certain assumptions, the thermal performance of buildings. However, the accuracy with which computer or laboratory simulations and other techniques can predict quantifiable economic and environmental performances of a building proposal vary widely. The degrees to which anyone can accurately predict unquantifiable social and cultural effects of a building proposal are even more varied. Claims of accuracy can lead to a spurious impression of legitimacy, as in the 'accurate' prediction of some aspects of a building's environmental performance being used to legitimate its design when other aspects that are predicted with far less accuracy, or simply ignored, may collectively be far more significant. As Aristotle reminds us,

> One should not require precision in all pursuits alike, but in each field precision varies with the matter under consideration and should be required only to the extent to which it is appropriate to the investigation. ... in order to prevent minor points assuming a greater importance than the major tasks.
>
> (Aristotle 1962: 1, 1098a)

The questions we as designers need to ask are 'is knowledge irrelevant because it is not accurate enough, or is it needlessly accurate?' and 'is a greater degree of accuracy important, even if this causes extra expense?' Answering these questions in a general context leads us to a concern with the adequacy and relevance of knowledge about design advice and the imposition of regulations.

Design advice

Sustainability is both a professional and a public concern, and there is much information available which sets out to *explain* how environmental aspects of sustainability relate to architecture and/or describe how design *should address* these issues. The pre-eminent source of such design advice is theory that aims to describe and explain the world (or aspects of the world) as it is, sometimes called *positive* theory because of its links to the modernist attitude of positivism (Lang 1987). Positive theory is likely to originate from building science and a tradition of research into material properties, lighting and energy use, or from physiology and the development of comfort theories. *Normative* theory states how design *ought* to address environmental issues according to positive theory. The approach to knowledge embodied by these techniques is that of the search for objective facts in a defined field, using research techniques such as physical and computer modelling, technical monitoring and statistical analysis. Degrees of accuracy and certainty are rarely clearly expressed. Instead the image associated with information generated using these techniques is that they provide a 'true' picture of the world.

Such theory results in prescriptions for what the designer should do[6] in the form of 'scientifically justified' rules of thumb, design guidelines, standards and regulations, manifestos and polemic that, it is suggested, will achieve a desired outcome if applied to the practice of design. Advice is often presented in ways that suggest it can be used independently of other design concerns. It is also often implied that appropriate solutions are 'measurably' better, demonstrated by determining how closely a design complies with a recognized image of an environmentally or economically (rarely culturally) appropriate solution, or by modelling its potential impact.

There are two principle kinds of design advice: that which focuses on the means used in design (processes or technologies), and that which focuses on the performance of a design while leaving means up to the decision-makers. In their manifestation as local, national or international regulations, they are usually described as prescriptive, where particular solutions are required to be implemented, or performance-based, where measurable performance criteria are set out and associated levels of achievement stated that are deemed to meet certain objectives.

Means-based advice: prescriptions and prototypes

Design advice and the critical evaluation of building proposals often address the *means* adopted to meet objectives. The advice explains 'how to' design and build appropriately: what procedures to follow and checks to make, what materials to use, where a building should be oriented, how to construct features that are held to have desirable characteristics. An evaluation of a design checks that these means have indeed been adopted in the design. The preparation and presentation of almost all such design advice or prescriptive evaluation checklists are based on a premise of universality. It is assumed that it is possible to present information about how environmental issues should be addressed in building design in terms of solutions that are not specific to a time, place or client. This creates a theoretical image that such information can be applied directly, or adapted, to a variety of design situations.

'Means-based' assessments are often suspect in terms of methodological transparency. Designs that do not conform with the acceptable lists may in fact be achieving the objectives, and where means-based assessment is given authority solutions tend to be limited to those on the lists. Compare this kind of advice with the more general images that architects use in their work. For example, a mental image of heat flow through materials may be far more beneficial than the knowledge of specific U-values of building components. The image might combine sensual aspects such as the feel of a masonry wall warmed by the sun in winter, or a metal sheet roof baking on a 40°C day. It could incorporate a sense of thickness, of durability, of appropriateness, and of availability – all helpful concepts for design. It may be related to technical information learnt as a student, overlaid with direct experience, information gleaned from the media and conversations with associates. The image is dynamic and constantly evolving, encompassing such things as visual, technical, emotional and affective issues, design conventions, common building practices, the designer's and client's values, and their experiences.

A good example is the body of design advice available in many countries that promotes what can be called the 'solar-efficient model' of house design. Since the 1970s, the solar-efficient model has been advocated in temperate climates (to the virtual exclusion of other models) as an appropriate way of addressing environmental issues in housing. It has been promoted through design advice such as design guides, environmental regulations, and journal articles, as well as in public awareness campaigns and through the education of several generations of building designers. The rationale of the solar-efficient model is essentially that the building structure is designed as a solar collector to reduce winter heating requirements and is heavyweight in construction to also reduce internal summer temperature swings. The solar-efficient strategy is based on using appropriate window area, orientation and shading for solar gain, in combination with internal mass and insulation to reduce unwanted heat loss and gain. The belief that a solar-efficient house is good for the environment is based on the idea that if the principles of the model are followed it is possible to design a house that can maintain internal comfort levels while using less purchased energy than a similar poorly designed house. Therefore, it is reasoned that a solar-efficient house can conserve resources and reduce pollution, particularly the emission of greenhouse gases. This image is so strong that the environmental friendliness of housing is likely to be judged according to whether a house (or house design) exhibits components of the solar-efficient model – such as concrete slab-on-ground floors, south facing windows (in the northern hemisphere, or north facing in the southern hemisphere) and massive walls – rather than its *actual* performance in operation.[7]

People are strangely absent from this image. They are assumed either as keen participants whose aims are identical to those expressed in the design advice or they are 'designed' out of participation because they cannot be trusted. For example, there is a strong image that it is the building itself that uses energy, not its occupants. Case studies and monitored projects rarely present a picture of the occupants and the way they relate to the use of energy. This contributes to the impression that issues to do with occupancy are not a major concern when considering the environmental aspects of design. The solar-efficient image, then, presents the idea that energy use is dependent on the form of the building fabric. This denies the significance of other determinants of energy use that are arguably far more important, including the occupants and their lifestyle, and even the *size* of the house. It downplays other images of houses that could be considered good for the environment; for example the small house, a house that is self-sufficient in energy, a house of low embodied energy, a house that uses recycled materials, a healthy house or one that allows an intimate and affectional relationship between the wider environment and the occupants. Actual performance is taken as influenced by 'uncontrolled' humans, and because their actual actions cannot be easily modelled they are ignored or standardized under an assumption that everyone acts the same way.

Ends-based advice: the performance concept

The concept of meeting needs is an integral component of most definitions of sustainable development, with a clear implication that needs can be determined independently of their context (Redclift 1994: 22). The idea of meeting needs has a resonance with thinking on building design, because the idea that buildings must satisfy users' *needs* has been part of this discourse over many years. An architect's images about a good design often relate to the satisfaction of the *users needs*, such as good lighting or places for community interactions in a shopping mall.

Perhaps the first attempt to define a comprehensive set of user needs was *The Basic Principles of Healthful Housing*, first published by the American Public Health Association's Committee on Hygiene of Healthful Housing in 1939 (APHA 1939). Four categories of needs were suggested as fundamental to good housing – physiological needs, psychological needs, protection against contagion, and protection against accidents. Adequate housing was judged by the degrees to which a number of conditions defined under each need category (eg. physiological needs – the provision for admission of direct light) were satisfied. This design thinking developed in the 1960s and 1970s into a taxonomy of needs under the banner of the performance concept. The development of such ideas at this time were seen as a means of:

- Providing a consistent framework for evaluating new building materials, elements and components
- Removing barriers to building innovation imposed by prescriptive building regulations
- Harmonizing the diverse building regulatory regimes that existed in Europe and North America.

In 1971 Gerard Blachère, then Director of the Centre Scientific et Technique du Bâtiment, Paris[8] said,

> Today the idea is being generally accepted that a satisfactory building should meet the end use which has been fixed explicitly or implicitly by the person who has ordered the building (and who pays for it). . . . [I]n other words the building should satisfy the user's requirements.
>
> (Blachère 1971)

'Performance-based' advice and evaluation begins by defining desired or required performances in relation to objectives, leaving the means to achieve those

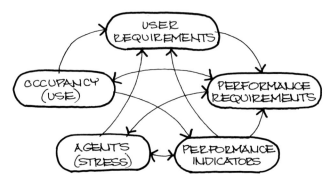

4.2 User requirements (drawn by Deborah White).

performances to be chosen by the designers. In operation, the performance concept centres on the idea that products, devices, systems or services can be described and their performances specified in terms of *performance requirements* without regard to their physical characteristics, design or the method of their creation. Inherent in the approach is the assumption that it is possible to describe 'performance' in a meaningful and generally universal way.

The *user requirement* is the essence of the performance concept (Figure 4.2). *Performance requirements* are qualitative statements describing goals of overall design outcomes or products and subsystems within the solution related to the *user requirement*. The act of satisfying a requirement is delegated to a *functional element*, usually a building component, including their aggregation into a whole building. A *performance requirement* is the 'user requirement expressed in terms of the performance of a product' and it is represented by a *performance indicator*. The performance indicator is any quantifiable measure that adequately represents the specific performance requirement, for example, temperature limits to describe comfort satisfaction. These provide quantitative statements of the desired attributes of a final design outcome and enable functional elements to be assessed in relation to *agents (stress)* that affect how a building behaves.

By the early 1980s the performance concept was formalized in two ISO standards, *ISO 6240 Performance Standards in Building – Contents and Presentation* (ISO 1980) and *ISO 6241 Performance Standards in Building – Principles for their Preparation and Factors to be Considered* (ISO 1984a). Fourteen fields of user requirements associated with a building and its component products were identified in the Standards: stability, fire safety, safety in use, air and water tightness, hygrothermal, air purity, acoustical, visual, tactile, anthropodynamic, hygiene, suitability of spaces for specific uses, durability and economic. The performance requirements were to be determined directly from a consideration of the users of the proposed building. While entirely human orientated, conceptual requirements could be derived from many different interests, including building users, building owners, and the community. The logic was essentially deductive and all possible designs could be conjectured and evaluated against the requirements. A formal definition of the performance concept was accepted as:

> An attempt to provide a framework within which it is possible to state the desired attributes of a material, component or system in order to fulfil the requirements of the intended user without regard to the specific means to be employed in achieving the results.
>
> (Wright 1970)

The key to its application was the identification of significant criteria that characterized the performance expected and the subsequent generation of methodologies for measuring how products, processes, or systems met these criteria. To explain this procedure of evaluation Haider and Khachaturian (1972) framed the performance concept in terms of a process of designing where candidate solutions are in turn subject to an evaluation process, scored and ranked by their ability to satisfy the performance criteria. Taken together, the performance requirements would appear to define much of the building design problem. The empirical evaluation against the accompanying performance criteria would then determine the range of possible solutions. But obvious issues are avoided such as, 'What happens if requirements conflict?' and 'What priority should we give to the various requirements?' These and other issues were behind the question asked by James Gross, of the US National Institute of Standards and Technology in his address opening an international conference on the performance concept:

> If the performance concept is so widely embraced philosophically, if the approach is so widely accepted intellectually, if the principles are easy to understand, if the methodology removes barriers to innovation, if the performance concept can aid in the production of buildings that perform better at less total cost, why isn't it universally applied?
>
> (Gross 1996)

The globalization of standards and regulations

The central answer to Gross's question lies in the fact that fundamentally the concept, in assuming that user requirements can be framed in universal terms, is flawed in a rather obvious way. It cannot in any real way account for the differences between peoples' preferences and expectations, their culture and society and the prevailing economic circumstances and capabilities. In other words, it does not allow for the unique problem definition that is essential for good, sustainable, architecture. Such an approach, far from being universal, would start by acknowledging that needs are socially constructed and that each society must define its needs in its own way.[9] International standards work counter to this imperative. Being generally derived from a European/North American perspective (because this is where the research is conducted) they adopt criteria in defining needs that often have little contextual relevance to the rest of the world, in particular countries of a different cultural and economic circumstance. For example, the application of ISO 7730 '*Moderate Thermal Environments – Determination of PMV and PPD Indices and Specification of the Conditions for Thermal Comfort*' (ISO 1984b) to building design in hot tropical climates would mean that a building would always be air conditioned.

Proper definition of the problem at hand is essential to achieving sustainable architecture. Yet, at least in Western societies, the belief in some universal application of building design principles often clouds this exigency. The issue is exacerbated when we consider issues associated with the international culture of architecture and the globalization of building industries introduced in Chapter 2, including the view that to an architect all architectures are intelligible, albeit conditioned by the practical necessity of coping with local variations and environments. Internationally agreed performance standards, and the international promotion of performance-based building codes, also promote normative and perhaps uncritical positions.[10] Legal systems are an expression of culture, and in many societies the regulation of building is part of that system. People insist on the need for regulation of an industry whose products can have an enormous impact on a society. Modern building regulations were implemented ostensibly in the interest of communities, with the initial objective of protecting health and safety, but also act to provide a level playing field for builders and others competing in the building industry. Other public and national interests that are aspects of sustainability, such as energy conservation, reduction in CO_2 emissions and safeguarding the environment, are now generally admitted as legitimately within the scope of building regulation. Issues such as quality control, consumer protection and the wider facets of environmental protection are being considered as future areas for regulation in many jurisdictions. But with the globalization of the building industry locally-derived building regulations are criticized as non-tariff barriers to international trade.[11] There are increasing calls to harmonize building regulations throughout the world and major international trade agreements support this view, in effect defining needs in some universal manner.[12] For example, signature countries to the GATT Agreement (1994) that followed the Uruguay Round of Multilateral Trade Negotiations, acceded to the *Agreement On Technical Barriers To Trade* which in the section on *Technical Regulations And Standards* says:

> 2.4 Where technical regulations are required and relevant international standards exist or their completion is imminent, Members shall use them, or the relevant parts of them, as a basis for their technical regulations except when such international standards or relevant parts would be an ineffective or inappropriate means for the fulfilment of the legitimate objectives pursued, for instance because of fundamental climatic or geographical factors or fundamental technological problems.
>
> (WTO, 1994)

At the same time, mandating performance standards for issues such as energy efficiency are seen as overly prescriptive and inflexible instruments of public policy that are likely to be an impediment to the introduction of sustainable design concepts and technologies.

Local contexts

Based on assumptions of good and bad, right and wrong, and desirable and undesirable, design advice is inherently value-laden (Lang 1987: 16). Its structure is not neutral and can profoundly influence the outcome, for example by the way it facilitates or obscures the ability to comprehend linkages and conflicts (Cole 1997: 184). The reductionist approach underlying most current guides, standards and regulations towards aspects of sustainability ignores the many contextual issues that have to do with good design (such as cultural, social, historical, and aesthetic concerns) and commonly concentrate on environmental factors in general, and resource use efficiency in particular. Because each design situation is unique, and virtually none is only an environment-related or a resource-related problem, no general design guide can validly provide a complete solution to a particular decision-making problem unless it provides sufficient information to enable us to be sure that the problem as defined in the guide is, in all relevant aspects, virtually identical to the one at hand. This is only likely to be the case for very narrow problems. So any design guide, book, code, standard or computer software that either prescribes a solution (that is, it tells us what to do) or assesses proposals against particular solutions (that is, by comparison, insinuates what to do), must be treated sceptically to ensure that the assumptions upon which it is based are really applicable. This involves checking for relevant objectives that are omitted, as well as checking that the explicit and implicit objectives that are addressed coincide with those relevant in the specific case. We are not implying that this means that they are not worth reading and using. Rather, it means that they should always be read and used from an informed and questioning standpoint, asking about absence or completeness, confusion, uncertainty and inaccuracy in the knowledge as it is presented and as it applies to the specific circumstance.

We shall take the example of the old quarter of Hanoi in Vietnam (Figure 4.1) to illustrate the application and import of these problems in a concrete situation (similar situations occur in other places and countries). The principal passive stakeholders in the old quarter are those people who live and work in the area, whose objectives centre on the myriad aspects of quality of life and for whom the knowledge that 'this is my traditional family house' and 'I have lived here since I was very young' are very important (Rees 1997). But this is an area of national and international significance as cultural heritage. The human stakeholders extend well beyond the area and, indeed, the country, and their objectives include maintaining and enhancing cultural heritage value (and, from a national and city-wide perspective, potential future tourist income from those who will come to see that heritage). The principal active stakeholders are planners, architects, government officials and politicians who make decisions about interventions in the area in major or minor ways. Some of these are local people, while some are overseas experts. In an architectural context the principal means are changes to the fabric and services of buildings, but the resources available to do so are limited. So the challenge of sustainability in this area is not just concerned with the repair of the decaying fabric of an individual building, but is more about refurbishing the body of a vital living organism in a way that the whole is sustainable.

The issues in the sustainability equation concern maintaining and enhancing social cohesion, the sense of place, family and social ties, together with preserving the historical character of the buildings, and creating a healthy, safe and economically vital environment. Architects have a role in this, bringing their professional skill to the task of improving physical conditions and reinforcing the sense of continuity and culture that the buildings of the area represent. In this task, the cultural constructions of sustainability within the discipline of architecture must meet the cultural constructions of sustainability held by the people of the area. The recognition that these constructions are likely to differ is central to developing designs that respond to the local situation. Satisfying the spiritual, economic, and material needs of people is a determining condition for sustainable architecture, and every decision concerning the design of a building must be sensitive to the culture, the resources, and the character of the place. The risk is that global standards, global modes of building and global processes will overwhelm the local context. This risk is enhanced as Vietnam, after many years of deprivation, attempts to improve the lot of its people in the modern world. While designers and designs may be superficially sensitive to the local context, the result can easily tend towards an international characterization of the local – old quarter of Hanoi (and innumerable other places) as theme park rather than a self-renewing neighbourhood. The area that has evolved and sustained itself since being first settled around 2000 years ago is about to enter a new phase. Whether it continues to be sustainable when the *needs* are, to a large extent, being determined beyond itself, is uncertain.

In this chapter we have approached design for a more sustainable architecture through the articulation of stakeholders, objectives and means, and positioned the role of design advice in relation to means and ends. In the Appendix to this book we offer a partial checklist of our own which is itself a kind of design advice, but which seeks to be explicit about stakeholders, objectives and means. This partial checklist – we make no claim that it is comprehensive – is structured by a system theory approach to architectural sustainability that we explore in the next chapter.

Notes

1 The terminology of this branch of decision-making theory tends to use passive and active subjects rather than stakeholders, and desired ends rather than objectives. Here we use the terms most likely to be familiar to architects.
2 Beach's theory sets out the role in decision-making of three images (the value, strategic and trajectory images – or images of why, what and how). Beach observes that 'right' here relates to the decision maker's own values, ethics, beliefs, and morals, not all of which are necessarily admirable (Beach 1990).

3 The term tacit knowledge is sometimes used for the body of unformalized knowledge that practitioners acquire.

4 This use of images can be illustrated by research about the way a group of Australian architects used environmental prototypes while designing houses for clients (Bennetts 2000). It became clear that these architects did not see themselves as using much environmental design advice at all. Indeed, some were vaguely apologetic about this (possibly in deference to what they imagined the researchers' viewpoint to be) and others were dismissive about the usefulness of much of the available information. Nonetheless, they obviously were aware of, and used, many theoretical concepts in their work and were designing environmentally thoughtful buildings. It appeared that rather than using design advice in a prescriptive or instrumental way, these architects worked with an image of what was embodied in such information and what this meant for their particular designs. They also referred to images from other sources that appeared to be useful during design, such as their previous experiences or knowledge of other buildings. They described their designs in a story-like way: setting the scene, introducing the main characters, outlining the aims and motivations (both the clients' and their own), strategies, and outcomes. These 'stories' incorporated a range of images. There are the clients' images of their future house (a 'dream house', something 'stylish and modern', something 'low cost that suited the site' and a house that has 'minimal impact'). There are images based on the clients' and architects' experiences of other places such as traditional cottages, project homes and dark villas. There are images of goals such as creating a house that is 'low energy', 'appropriate to place' or 'light and bright'. The architects referred to the use of such images in communication with their clients, and used them frequently as they described their designs during the interviews. Images are used to connect design concepts to specific experiences, emotions or examples such as the feeling of heavyweight construction, the need for air conditioning in particular climates and building types, how specific rooms may be used, and what external appearance is desirable. Images were also used to link goal to strategies.

5 Current theory on decision-making regarding buildings and built environments comes from a huge range of disciplines, as well as from the narrative knowing which we use in our everyday dealings with the world. Discussing environmental discourse, Teymur (1982) shows how this Babel of theory and practice interacts and clashes to produce many confusions and other difficulties affecting problem definition; he also shows how many of these difficulties are ignored in practice, though this is perhaps shown even more clearly by the demonstrated feasibility of producing good buildings without the aid of any comprehensive body of widely accepted theory. Many theorists have noted this absence of comprehensive theory (for example Lynch 1984 Chapter 2 and Lang 1987: 12), and though some claim to be filling that gap, their claims are not widely accepted. Despite this lack, some aspects of decision-making regarding buildings are treated in ways which involve well-developed and well-accepted bodies of theory – consider structural engineering theory, involving mathematical modelling of the behaviour of structures in response to forces or loads.

6 Although derived from a 'scientific' tradition, science itself does not deal with prescriptions for creation (Johnson 1994: 19).

7 For example, a number of local councils in Australia have developed policies related to the energy efficiency or environmental sustainability of housing that essentially consist of a checklist of design attributes of this kind (Glendinning 1996; Sutherland Shire Council 1997).

8 In 1996 Prof Blachère was presented with a CIB shield with the inscription 'The International Council for Building Research, Studies and Documentation honors the unique contribution by Gerard Blachère to furthering the worldwide frontiers of building science in The Performance Concept in Building'.

9 Hillier and Penn note that, for building design problems, performances (desired ends) need to be understood in relation to the particular design problem, and

that this has implications for the means which should be used to address those performances.

> Buildings and built environments must satisfy a range of functional criteria – structural, environmental, economic, social, organizational, visual, and so on. These functional criteria are independent, in that they are nothing like each other but are interactive in that when you change a building to get one right you may make something else go wrong. This creates two knowledge problems in the making and managing of buildings. One is integrating knowledge of the product and its functioning into a better understanding of the buildings as a complex whole. The other is integrating the process to create the virtuous circle of progressive product improvement through feedback from user experience. In this paper we argue that these are aspects of the same problem, and have a common solution. The solution starts from a very simple observation: that the different functional criteria affect each other only through the building. It follows that to see how they relate, we must therefore take a building centred rather than a discipline centred view of buildings and how they function.
>
> (Hillier and Penn 1994: 332)

If performances must be understood in relation to particular building design problems, how can they be predefined?

10 All evaluations need to be adjustable according to national and regional conditions. This does not necessarily contradict the moves to develop international standards. It is necessary to determine where it makes sense to formulate international standards and where it is unworkable and improper to do so because of the regional and cultural variations.

11 Greg Foliente noted that:

> The worldwide interest in the development of performance-based building codes is primarily driven by the need to address the difficulties posed by current prescriptive codes and standards to:
>
> (1) cost-optimize building construction,
> (2) introduce product or system and process innovation, and
> (3) establish fair international trading agreements.
>
> The prescriptive or deemed-to-comply building codes that are currently enforced in most countries around the world are major non-tariff trade barriers that inhibit building and construction trade. To address this issue, the World Trade Organization (WTO) has included Clause 2.8 of the Agreement on Technical Barriers to Trade (WTO 1997), which states that: 'Wherever appropriate, Members shall specify technical regulations based on product requirements in terms of performance rather than design or descriptive characteristics'. Member economies that are signatories to the WTO General Agreement on Tariffs and Trade (GATT) have therefore committed themselves, whether wittingly or not, to the use of performance requirements in evaluating a product's fitness for purpose and in accepting new and/or innovative products in their market, or to state it briefly, to use the language of performance in trade.
>
> (Foliente 1998)

12 It is now well accepted that the performance language and tools can become the basis for harmonization and globalization of the building market, and be a means for eliminating barriers to trade (Gross 1996).

5 Systems

Decision theory articulates objectives and means, but does not address the links between them. When we concern ourselves closely with the performance of designs, including the inputs of resources that they require and the waste products that they generate, we need to understand more about how buildings and the wider world interact and behave. Because this is complex and the potential scope enormous, we need some way of structuring the problem. The way humans generally tackle complex situations is to try to break them down into a collection of smaller, more manageable parts.[1] Indeed, we noted in Chapter 1 that one credo of modern living is reductionism, the breaking down of a problem into simpler units and the belief that if we can study and understand directly these simple units, we can reassemble the whole structure in a logical fashion. The effectiveness of this strategy explains a large part of the success of modern science and applied technology, and we can look at a sustainable architecture in this way too; while we want to recognize the limitations of the scientific view, we do not want to neglect the benefits. Much of the way we look at sustainability issues is predicated on this scientific approach. As we have seen in the previous chapter, many of the needs or ends that should be met as a necessary condition for a sustainable future are defined in scientific terms. While this approach certainly has strengths, many critics (see for example Redclift 1994) have pointed out that it also highlights the limitations of the scientific view because the way we structure a problem can never be neutral. It will be conditioned by our circumstances, our values and ethical positions, as well as the implicit boundaries between our knowledge and our ignorance. Because of this limitation, the elements of the structure will inevitably be contrivances based on our existing understanding and will not be entirely unbiased. In this chapter we examine what useful knowledge lies at the intersection between building design and sustainability. To begin this examination we first look at the way this knowledge about buildings is (and may be) structured into a logical world view based on the theory of system behaviour.

System theory deals with relationships between parts. Although it is inherently reductionist, the emphasis is on trying to understand these relationships rather than simply the reduction into parts. It is widely accepted as a useful way of looking at the world and provides a conceptual framework to structure sustainability assessment.

A systems view

'A system is a set of inter-dependent processes and the world is full of them' (Markus, Whyman *et al.* 1972: 2). Traditional scientific thinking is founded on the logical exploration of identifiable relationships of cause and effect. The connection is direct; as input variables to a process change, outputs change without any intervening mediation. Many real life conditions are of a different, more complex, kind in which the parts are not significantly linked to each other except with reference to the whole. The theory of systems developed as a basis for dealing with such phenomena. In his influential book *Environment, Power, and Society*, Howard Odum pointed out that although we may understand individual mechanistic processes, a broad view connecting these bits together is required to appreciate 'larger wholes and patterns'. To achieve this he recommended taking a systems view.

> We can begin a systems view of the earth through the macroscope of the astronaut high above the earth. From an orbiting satellite, the earth's living zone appears to be very simple . . . The biosphere is the largest ecosystem, but the forests, the seas, and the great cities are systems also. The great chunks of nature also have subsections and zones which are organized by their physical processes and organisms into systems of function.
>
> (Odum 1970: 11)

In a similar way a 'view' of an entire building may be disaggregated into physical and societal processes that form complex subsystems of the whole system. Ludwig von Bertalanffy, generally considered to be the founder of general system theory, defines a system simply as a set of elements standing in interrelation among themselves and with the environment (von Bertalanffy 1971). How a system is delimited and described is not intrinsic to the assembly of elements but depends on the observer's viewpoint in defining the purpose and activities of the system. The resolution level (degree of detail) adopted, and whether the system is regarded as real or conceptual, will reflect that viewpoint.

Adopting the most common terminology, systems may be classified as closed or open. A closed system is one in which all the component processes interact only with one another and are not influenced by other external processes. An open system does interact with other systems external to itself. The states that can be reached in a closed system are completely determined by its structure, whereas those in an open system depend also on corresponding states in the other systems or environment with which it interacts. A closed system will have no impact outside of itself. A building is an open system. Katz and Kahn (1966) list the characteristics of open systems as:

- The import of energy or information from the environment,
- The transformation of that energy into some form that is characteristic of the system,

5.1 Longevity: weathered stone and timber walls of the barns at Highfield House, in Tasmania, Australia from 1928. They were built following the appropriation of land by Colonial authorities and its allocation to the Van Diemen's Land Company. A detail appears on the front cover of this book (photographer Antony Radford).

- The export of the product into the environment, and
- The re-energizing of the system from sources in the environment.

Environmental sustainability (that is, the sustainability of the 'outside' environment within which an open system exists) can be described quite simply by two rules:[2]

- Input rule: Inputs to a system must be constrained within the ability of the wider system to continue to provide the same inputs without degradation.
- Output rule: Emissions from a system must be contained within the ability of the wider system to continue to assimilate them without degradation.

A common aim in sustainable architecture is to create 'more closed' and 'less open' systems in buildings, by feeding back (for example, through recycling) and minimizing import of materials and export of waste, so that the input and output rules are easier to satisfy because there is less of both.

It is axiomatic that any system can be decomposed into subsystems. In defining the boundaries of a system, then, we are implicitly specifying a particular resolution level and classifying all systems of greater scope as merging into the environment, and all systems below that level as elements that do not require to be further analysed. The scope of the pertinent system is determined by the broadest purpose of interest, since the system boundaries must include all significant channels whereby the consequences of an action are apparent or brought back to influence future action (Forrester 1968). To construct and describe a system or subsystem it is necessary to frame the kinds of behaviour that are of interest and the way the whole operates. More often than not the system definition is a conjecture, a mental picture about elements and their connections rather than something more resolved.[3] While we still do not understand many well accepted systems in the natural world, and many systems relevant to building are only described in broad narrative terms, they are nevertheless valuable aids to understand (if only partly) observed behaviours and to anticipate future outcomes.

Buildings as systems

Much theory on the application of instrumental knowledge in building design assumes a systems approach.[4] When we look at a billboard on the construction site of a large building, we see the structuring of knowledge into systems and subsystems in the list of consultants and specialists associated with the project. Like it or not, the fact that buildings are being constructed using this approach is a validation that such a way of dividing knowledge has some justification. We can therefore ask the question 'What would be a suitable system model for the purpose of structuring knowledge to evaluate the performance of a building in terms of its sustainability; in terms of satisfying *needs?*' In Chapter 1 we noted that thinking about sustainable development is often represented in terms of three conceptual subsystems – environmental, economic and sociocultural, the triple bottom line. Sometimes this representation is tied to an image that a sustainable development is like a three legged stool; fail in one subsystem, take one leg away, and the quest for a sustainable development falls over. While this system model might be appropriate to consider general development issues, when we get to the level of actual buildings two elements (subsystems) are absent – the building and the building users. A suitable building system model

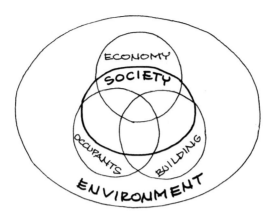

5.2 Systems/subsystems view (drawn by Deborah White).

should be capable of dealing with the *needs* of all relevant stakeholders – human and non-human. If we impose a further criterion that there is more or less a distinguishable body of knowledge associated with each subsystem, then an appropriate building-centred system model might be constructed from the relationships between five subsystems, (Figure 5.2) such that:

- The *Environment* subsystem uniquely contains the subsystem *Society*.
- Subsystems of *Economics*, *Occupants* and *Building* overlap both the *Environment* and *Society* subsystems.
- The subsystems *Economics*, *Occupants* and *Building* have positive intersections.

Our aim in using such a construction is to bring relevant knowledge from the subsystem disciplines into something of a conceptual whole. Needs can be ascribed to parts within each subsystem, and these will relate to the inputs and outputs of that subsystem. However, each subsystem cannot be said to be an entirely separate entity. Overlaps and interconnections obviously occur and understanding these is just as important as understanding the behaviour within each subsystem. For example, the adverse impact of emissions produced by a building, such as the off-gasing of materials, may have an effect on the health of the occupants, the economic subsystem in terms of productivity, as well as the surrounding environmental system. Similarly the social relevance of a building is integrally bound to how it meets stakeholder needs and its economic viability. At this stage, we place no particular significance on the ordering of the subsystems or the prominence that should be ascribed to each. What we need to investigate first is what elements will comprise the inputs and outputs to each subsystem and how will these provide us with pointers to a sustainable design. In the following sections we shall examine each of these subsystems in turn.

The environment

Even taking a minimal, instrumental position, the need to consider environmental impact is an indisputable aspect of producing sustainable architecture. The question is, however, exactly what are we referring to here: the greenhouse effect, the thinning of the ozone layer, carcinogens produced by building products, heavy metals pollution of waterways, the mounting problems of waste disposal or conserving precious water resources? Or should our concern be with the exhaustion of mineral resources, the long-term storage of radioactive waste or the survival of trees and frogs? Both emissions in the way of pollution and extraction are forms of impact on the environment and are inputs and outputs to the subsystem. In the historical development of the environment discourse, these two aspects of environmental impact are generally treated as separate issues. Emissions involve the release of a substance into the environment, while the use of raw materials involves the extraction of substances from the environment for application in buildings.

Emissions

Chemical or physical agents (substances, noise, etc.) may be released into the environment as the result of human activities associated with buildings. Some emissions may effect people, fauna or flora directly or contribute to a gradual disturbance of the earth's ecosystem. For example, emissions from a metal foundry (even within legal limits) close to a residential area have been known to contribute to the incidence of asthma in the local neighbourhood; carbon dioxide released by the burning of fossil fuels could contribute to global warming; toxic waste from the manufacture of some building materials and released to a drainage system that eventually flows to the sea have led to a steady loss of biodiversity in fish and aquatic vegetation. Other emissions, like noise and stench, can simply cause annoyance and discomfort in everyday life. The more prominent of the environmental issues attributable to buildings (resulting from their manufacture and operation) are: the greenhouse effect, depletion of the ozone layer, smog, toxins (human and environmental), waste disposal, and radioactivity.

The greenhouse effect

This is caused by gases that block outgoing infra-red radiation from the earth; this effect alters the heat balance and could result in dangerous (to humans and many other species) climatic changes. We shall focus on this issue in Chapter 6.

Depletion of the ozone layer

The ozone layer in the earth's stratosphere absorbs ultraviolet radiation (UV). Excessive UV radiation is potentially damaging to plant and animal life (ultraviolet radiation, for example, is one cause of human and animal skin cancers). The best known of the ozone depleting substances are a range of manufactured chemicals known as the chlorofluorocarbons (CFCs), particularly CFC-12 (freon). Since the 1920s CFCs have been used for a number of applications in buildings such as the manufacture of plastic foams, in the cooling coils of refrigerators and air conditioners, in fire extinguishing systems, and as solvents for cleaning. Once discharged into the atmosphere, these chemicals take around 20 years to migrate to the ozone layer and then, under the action of sunlight, they break down and release free chlorine that tends to destroy the ozone layer. An international treaty, the 1987 Montreal Protocol on Substances that Deplete the Ozone Layer, is aimed at eliminating the use of the most damaging ozone depleting chemicals.

Smog

In summer smog can be caused by the presence of nitrogen oxides and carbohydrates in the air in combination with sunlight. Smog is harmful to people, and to flora and fauna; it can also cause serious economic damage to crops. In winter, concentrations of SPM (small particulate matter) and SO_2 (sulphur dioxide) can cause respiratory problems in people.

Toxins

Many substances discharged into the air, water and soil from the manufacture and operation of buildings are poisonous to human beings, other animals, plants and to their supporting ecosystems. Illness related to Indoor Air Quality (IAQ) has become more common and an increasing public concern. Toxins may enter the body through inhalation, ingestion and skin contact. Many common items found in buildings can release chemical fumes. Some volatile sources are obvious, for example adhesives and paints. There are also less obvious sources such as treated woods, laminates, carpets, wall coverings and spores from fungi and moulds. A principal source of fumes is from volatile organic compounds, (VOCs) which become a gas or vapour at normal temperatures or under the influence of heat. These compounds are found in many common building products. Exposure to toxins may result in specific illness such as irritation of the mucous membranes or skin, but is often manifest as non-specific illness such as headache, fatigue or difficulties in concentrating.

Waste disposal

Many countries face an urgent shortage of suitable sites for solid waste disposal. Inappropriate disposal of waste products can result in the pollution of the air, soil or waterways.

Radioactivity

Many people see the dangers posed by possible accidents in nuclear power plants and the storage problems of radioactive waste as potentially the most hazardous of the threats faced by humans.

Extractions

The predicted depletion of the earth's stocks of fossil fuels and certain ore and mineral resources is a particular concern in most literature about sustainable building. In this respect, it is useful to distinguish between non-renewable and renewable resources.

Non-renewable resources

The fossil fuels and uranium that power the operation of buildings and provide the energy to manufacture, transport and erect the materials and components used to construct the buildings in the first place (the embodied energy), are theoretically plentiful yet there are practical and economic limits to extracting these resources from the earth. In a similar way the stocks of some mineral deposits and metal ores appear to have been decreasing rapidly in the last century. The issue is probably not if or when these resources will 'run out', but rather how quickly and at what speed can substitutes be introduced. In practice the depletion of fuel, mineral and ore stocks will have a significant economic impact. Costs increase as lower-grade deposits are mined and material has to be shipped further around the globe. The use of lower grade ores also leads to higher energy use, more waste and more emission of pollutants. Repeated recycling of metals has the potential ultimately to lead to a lower quality material, unless more energy is used for refining and processing.[5]

Renewable resources

Renewable sources are by definition inexhaustible, but the production potential of renewable resources such as wood is limited. The uses of renewable energy sources like solar power, wind, tide and wave energy are being implemented, but rather slowly. The primary reason for this is that, at present, non-renewable sources of energy are less expensive for consumers. But another obvious issue that needs to be considered is the degrees to which technical systems that capture renewable energy, such as solar photovoltaic panels (PV) for generating electricity and their associated equipment and circuitry, may themselves require energy and rare minerals in their manufacture. There has to be a life cycle benefit but 25 years ago PV systems, while heavily promoted, took more energy to make than they would generate over an expected lifetime. While PV technology has improved, depending on the actual cell manufacturing technology (monocrystalline silicon or polycrystalline silicon) and the climate condition, a photovoltaic module may, over an operating lifetime of 25 years, produce only two times or up to twenty times the energy that it took to make it.

Clean water is vital to life as well as the construction and operation of buildings. In many areas of the world this is perhaps the most critical of all resources that we extract from the environment system. The increasing demands for water storage facilities and associated destruction of natural areas, the problems of over-extracting ground water supplies, the problems of ground salinity and the increasing costs of requirements to decontaminate polluted sources, all point to this being a critical issue for the design of sustainable buildings, where building in this case also includes the related landscape.

Social and cultural relevance

Cultural diversity is humankind's contribution to maintaining the delicate balance in the variety of contextual circumstances throughout the globe. Maintaining this cultural diversity must be seen as an integral component of a sustainable architecture, because history would seem to show that variety among human societies is the source of adaptation and of innovation. The sustainability of culture as tradition depends upon humans' capacity to learn and to transmit knowledge to succeeding generations. But tradition in response to the conditions of everyday life is not a static system:

> It is a myth to think of traditions as impervious to change. Traditions evolve over time, but also can be quite suddenly altered or transformed . . . they are invented and reinvented . . . As the influence of tradition and custom shrink on a world-wide level, the very basis of our self-identity – our sense of self – changes. In more traditional situations, a sense of self is sustained largely through the stability of the social positions of individuals in the community. Where tradition lapses, and life-style choice prevails, the self isn't exempt. Self-identity has to be created and recreated on a more active basis than before.
>
> (Giddens 1999b)

The rebuilding after a disastrous earthquake in 1956 of villages in the Greek Cyclades island of Thera (otherwise known as Santorini) illustrates the desire to be socially and culturally relevant. Following discussions with local people, new houses maintained the original scale and form of building, although replacing the traditional *tephra* (*pozzalana*) with reinforced concrete and ordering them in neat efficient rows rather than the picturesque apparent disorder of accretion over time (Figure 5.3) (Oliver 2000, Radford and Clark 1972). In later years regulations and community pressure have continued this vocabulary of forms in restoration and new building, in at least a part of the island. Indeed, the principle of development as 'repairing the city' is literal with many rebuilt buildings. Changes in economic circumstances affect the sustainability of cultures. The chief industry of Thera has shifted from fishing and agriculture to tourism. Regeneration is now driven by this industry. Many of the dwellings are now second homes of Athenians or rented to tourists, but the architecture helps to sustain at least a sense of continuity in the culture[6] while still accommodating the radical changes that economic and other factors have inevitably caused (Figure 5.4).

5.3 Sociocultural sensitivity: the main town of Thera (Santorini) perched at the edge of a volcanic crater sunk into the Aegean Sea. Many of the buildings have been rebuilt or built new after an earthquake in 1956 (photographer Antony Radford).

5.4 Continuing the themes of the vernacular: houses built on Thera in the 1990s (with solar hot water systems) (photographer Antony Radford).

The social and cultural relevance of architecture, then, is a relevance to societies and cultures that are themselves always changing. These societies and cultures are not necessarily geographically based, and relevance is not necessarily achieved simply by following regional styles.

In line with the notion of multiple fields of significance introduced in Chapter 2, a client or client group can be framed as the local people with their own (very) local culture, requiring their own architecture for their sustainability. Indeed, international business is a non-geographic entity with its own global culture, and contemporary corporate architecture (much the same throughout the world) can be seen as reflecting the desire of this cultural group to see its values and ambitions manifest in its architecture. In this sense, international corporate architecture helps to sustain the culture of international business.

The occupants

The well-being, health and safety of a building's occupants and all those potentially effected by a building is a primary goal of a sustainable architecture. For example, a reasonable level of safety against structural collapse is an obvious necessity for sustainable architecture. Health goals, on the other hand, relate to all issues dealing with the long-term health of the occupants and passers-by. This subsystem also includes factors that, although not a direct threat to life, are concerned with the satisfaction users have with the building, its spaces and conditions. This involves notions of comfort (or minimizing discomfort) as well as protecting physical property within and around a building. As we have seen in Chapter 4, performance-based design advice and building codes constructed around the performance concept attempt to deal with this issue by establishing a priori a range of performance indicators to measure the satiation of the human needs deemed necessary for a sustainable building.

Economic performance

Issues of the allocation of resources in time and in space are central to realizing a sustainable architecture. By time we mean the choice between now or later, as a choice between the present or future generations. By space we mean the choice between here or elsewhere, as a choice between satisfying our own desires (perhaps well beyond basic needs) or the needs of others (Redclift 1994).

Sustainable economic performance is concerned both with resource allocations between projects (which projects are appropriate and should proceed) and resource allocation within a project (for example the choice of particular products and services). The individual elements of economic activity in a society concerned with such decision-making, such as output (goods, services, asset production, etc.) and input (materials, labour, capital, etc.), can take many forms and are influenced by many factors. Capitalist societies with market-based economies are, however, structurally dependent on one factor – capital accumulation. For architecture to be economically sustainable, individual projects in general must show a positive net capital benefit or benefit/cost ratio, or put simply, there must be a profit or imputed profit. While this point is obvious, it is conspicuously absent in most of the discussions and analysis concerning sustainable building design. Capital accumulation (or profit making) provides the foundation for state taxation revenues, continuing employment and for future investments. Yet many see economic growth based on short-term imperatives, a materialistic society driven by what they see as capitalist greed, as the reason of environmental and social problems:

> The root cause of the mess lies in an overwhelming emphasis on consumption and the route to human happiness and economic growth as the means of achieving it. . . . Economic growth in the conventional sense is the problem . . . its pursuit damages the environment, leads to social injustice, and is detrimental to real economic development.
>
> (Smith *et al.* 1998: 210)

When economists discuss sustainability they tend to fall into one of two camps. The first, taking a neo-classical view, see the conditions for a sustainable future as economic growth through competitive markets, deregulation, privatization and integration into global economies. The others tend to emphasize abandoning economic growth as a measure of a society's success, and focus instead on equity, reducing poverty, encouraging resource conservation, ecological limits, and regulation as the way ahead. The features of these two views is illustrated in Table 5.1, where they are seen as promoting sustainability in either a weak or a strong way.

A key difference in the two views goes to the heart of the sustainability debate and revolves around the notion of discounting as 'revaluing a future event, condition, service or product to give a present equivalent (*present value*)'(Price 1993: 4). Discounting implies giving more weight to the present than the future. Discounting the value of a coal deposit, for example, means that it is more valuable to the present generation and encourages its immediate use without endowing compensation to the future for the depletion of the resource.

While discounting provides certain theoretical (and perhaps moral) difficulties, at the operational building design level, a pragmatic view of economic sustainability is to accept the observation made by Newell and Paterson (1998) that 'it is generally only those environmental initiatives that do not threaten the interests and routines of industrial capitalism that succeed', and to act accordingly. For specific projects, individuals, companies and governments may legitimately adopt their post-tax rate of return at an acceptable level of risk and liquidity as a discount rate to assess the viability of investment options (Price 1993: 67).

The building

This subsystem is concerned with the human ownership needs that relate to the service life of a building and its components, and questions about the longevity

Table 5.1 Economic views and prospects for sustainable development

Very weak to weak sustainability	*Strong to very strong sustainability*
Economic growth rather than income transfers to equalize wealth	Rapid progress towards more efficient and frugal use of natural resources
Free markets in conjunction with technological progress will ensure manufactured capital of at least equal value will take the place of natural capital	Reduced scale of economy (and population). Existing stock of natural capital maintained and enhanced because the functions it performs cannot be duplicated by manufactured capital
Rules/regulations inappropriate, providing all costs are considered then the best interests are served by undertaking investments that provide the highest returns	Mandatory targets, incentives, regulatory structures
Does accept some critical thresholds for certain natural (environmental) capital	Objects to views that neglect critical physical limits on the use of environmental capital
Net Present Value (NPV) the key test of projects – chosen for highest yield compared to next best alternative	Generally opposes the conventional view of discounting in environmental decision-making
Maintain and increase total capital stock to be passed to next generation	Demands a bold approach towards alleviating poverty. Makes inter-generational equity a prime goal through resource conservation
Priority to medium term issues – soil erosion, contaminated water, clean air	Tends to look at longer term problems – biodiversity and global warming
Resources exploited now will raise welfare, and in developing countries this is the key to slowing population growth	Advocates wealth redistribution by reducing consumption in rich nations, direct transfers (subsidies) to reduce poverty, repairing environmental degradation
Technology provides the opportunity to increase welfare in the face of shrinking capital stock	An emphasis on reduced technology, soft energy paths, appropriate technology

performance of the constructed facility. It concerns questions of serviceability and durability. In the language of life cycle asset management, longevity performance is concerned with 'optimizing the value of a built asset throughout its programming, design, construction, maintenance, repair, renewal, and disposal phases' (Lacasse and Vanier 1996). For designers involved with creating sustainable buildings this points to the need to consider maintenance, replaceability and likely associated costs in the selection of components and materials. Designing for the life cycle of a building means balancing the present requirements against the uncertainty of future possible requirements.

The life cycle of a building

If we change even a small part of any subsystem, it is likely to have consequences throughout the whole system. For example, a seemingly small increase in required lighting levels in buildings (for safety reasons) might require more electricity to be generated. This in turn may require more coal (depending on the means of electricity generation). Its mining will cause more landscape degradation and its burning will cause more CO_2 to be produced. It is possible that there will be financial implications – good for some, bad for others – with resulting social and cultural effects. While we can use the system model to examine how design decisions will influence the state of the system, changes in the balance to the system will also occur naturally over time. These can be considered by looking at the life cycle of a building. This can usually be broken down into four distinct stages:

- The production of the building, including initiation and design, the manufacture of materials and components, and their assembly;
- The use of the building, with its requirements for operation and maintenance;
- The renovation/rehabilitation/recycling of the building, which parallels the production process;
- The demolition of the building, with the reuse or waste of materials and components.

All of these have to do with designing, because at each stage decisions are made that will affect subsequent outcomes and possibilities. Few of these decisions are straightforward. The following sections explain aspects of this complexity.

The production of buildings

The production of buildings includes the design and construction processes, with the origin and processing of materials, transport, and operations in design offices and on site. An environmental audit of materials will serve as an example of the complexity of the issues that arise. This may take the form of a detailed analysis by specialists or simply a mental check by an architect using the best information that is readily available. The analysis typically takes into account the following 'cradle-to-grave' steps (Sylvan and Bennett 1994: 45):

- Sites affected
- Processing impacts
- Product impacts.

This is usually problematic. Holland and Holland (1995) describe the complexity facing designers with the seemingly narrow problem of deciding what sort of timber to specify for house framing in the Australian state of New South Wales – imported or local, plantation or regrowth natural forest. Apart from the issues of price and ease of construction, other concerns relate to environmental impacts (wildlife conservation, soil conservation, water quality and the global carbon budget), energy consumption (embodied and operational) and economics (related to balance of payments and regional employment). Most houses in

Australia are stud-framed in one of four materials: steel, Australian hardwood, Australian planted softwood, or American Oregon softwood. Steel requires considerable energy in its manufacture, and there is a big hole left where the ore has been extracted. Australian hardwood comes from natural forests that support a multitude of flora and fauna. The sawmillers claim that they regenerate naturally, but there is some doubt about this. Australian softwood is pine, a non-indigenous tree that grows in planted forests with very restricted biodiversity. We don't find koalas and kangaroos in pine forests. American Oregon comes from forests that provide the habitat for a rare species of spotted owl. Holland and Holland (1995) concluded that the most ecologically friendly option depended on one's view of the relative significance of such non-commensurable matters as global warming and numbers of owls. Probably the best choice was Australian planted softwood, but only if these plantations are developed on reclaimed farmland rather than cleared natural forests. But there is another catch here: pine is a very tasty meal for termites, and is therefore commonly treated itself or the ground around is treated with long-lasting chemicals of varying toxicity. The ecologically sound answer therefore involves changing construction practices to one of the greener (and generally more expensive, and in narrow terms less effective) options for avoiding termite damage.

Other choices of materials involve similar judgements and decisions based on limited information. Rainforest timbers are used in construction. If their use in construction, the highest value market for them, is eliminated, then whatever future value rainforests are perceived to have in the areas they exist is also eliminated. No local economic argument remains against clearing and burning to make way for cattle ranches.

The choice of finishes can also present difficulties. Carpet may harbour dust mites and cause problems for asthma sufferers, but alternatives such as polyurethane sealed, formaldehyde glued timber floors are not universally considered trouble-free. Plastics, leather, aluminium, rubber, paints, indeed most materials, raise some kind of issue connected with the environmental impact of their production, the 'rights' of animals, human health, effects of mining, or other factors. Often there is an element of recursion: an audit of the material requires an audit for the plant and infrastructure necessary to produce the material. Even a radical restructuring in our economic system so that the cost of a building and its energy requirements represented the real cost (including environmental costs) to society and the world is problematic. We do not know what those costs are, and in any case they involve judgements about the relative importance of different environmental factors for which there are no widely accepted models.

Using and maintaining buildings

While they exist, the impact of buildings on the environment follows from their very presence (noise, shading, wind effects and visual impact), the energy and resources imported for their operation when in use (electricity, gas, water), and the waste products (water, garbage) exported from them.

We now know a number of design features aimed at reducing energy require-ments in many situations: higher insulation to walls and windows, solar heating of water, avoiding air leakage, avoiding (where possible) air conditioning, using high-efficiency lighting. Cutting energy use would not seem difficult, but we must be aware of side effects. For example, the experience in the UK of a doubling of the number of children with asthma in recent years has been attributed in part to sealed-up houses.[7] With the chimneys and 'inefficient' unsealed windows of the past there was usually enough ventilation in a house, and generally far too much.

The cultural dimension is even harder to manage. Anyone who travels will have noticed that buildings in cold climates are heated to higher temperatures than those to which buildings in hot climates are cooled. In New York during summer one has to carry a jacket to put on in the air-conditioned buildings. This has to do with culture, not comfort. And one cannot transfer assumptions about building use between times and cultures, and people do not always re-spond as one would expect. In many countries there is now a general expecta-tion to dress lightly, whereas in the nineteenth century the fashionable layering of clothes meant that comfort was maintained in winter even with the limita-tions of the technology of the time.

We also know a number of practices that reduce the demand for piped water: the use of water collected on site, and the storage and reuse of wastewater. Water can be collected off the roof, but manufacturers of some colour coated steel roofing sheets do not recommend its use where rainwater is collected for drinking, while some planning control authorities do not allow bright, shiny uncoloured steel sheeting to be used for aesthetic reasons. The collected water can be stored in rainwater tanks, but tests have shown that many Australian domestic water tanks contain dangerous levels of micro-organisms. Surface water can be retained on site in underground aquifers, but there is a risk of pollution of an important water source by allowing water that has washed over the oil and dirt of urban streets and driveways to mix with the natural aquifer system. Used domestic water can be filtered and reused in WC cisterns, and then treated through the public sewage system, or used in the garden, but this relies on householders avoiding the use of detergents. Reducing consumption of drinkable water by means of grey-water recycling and water saving appliances may be desirable from an environmental point of view, but this recycling can also have secondary economic and social consequences. This is because in coun-tries where water supplies are provided by commercial organizations the reality is that the water companies depend on the amount of water they sell to main-tain profitability. Water saving measures may lead to increases in water charges. The question is, who should pay for this increase? Also, if consumers use less water, the flow rates in the sewerage reticulation system will reduce. Because the system will not be flushed efficiently, solid waste and accompanying micro-organisms will increase. To avoid this, the utility authority will have to intro-duce additional water to flush the system. The result could well be that more water in total is used. What these examples emphasize is that all measures to reduce the environmental impact of buildings must also take into account the wider ramifications.

Demolition and recycling of buildings and their materials

Our society does not in general consider as a first option the reuse of building sites, let alone buildings or materials. Land in many countries is still being used as if it were a disposable resource to be taken from agriculture or nature and 'developed'. Only rarely is this process reversed; indeed, in the unlikely event that it was so, the legacies of the years of development will often make that land unfit for farming or recreation. Contaminated soil has to be moved elsewhere or sealed away under another round of building.

Most buildings have relatively short life-spans – 1960s and 1970s buildings are already being demolished, and the Japanese housing industry works on a premise of demolition and rebuilding every generation, with an expected life of about twenty years. The former is partly due to poor standards of construction and insufficient knowledge about the new construction techniques, the latter mainly for cultural reasons, where houses have been seen as a commodity to be chosen from samples at a 'house shop' and installed on the purchaser's site. How does one address this? Seek to make the houses more flexible, so that the owners will not wish to demolish and replace them (the 'long life, loose fit' alternative)? Seek to change the culture of a consumerist society where waste and replacement keeps an industry (and employment) going? Seek to make the materials in the house recyclable, so that the cycle is maintained but is less wasteful?[8]

Ideally, materials should be recyclable and ultimately (preferably after many cycles of use) degradable back into the environment. Traditional materials usually perform better in this regard than processed ones, and may perform well in other ways. David Lea comments:

> Materials that grow on or lie close to the living surface of the planet, as close as possible to the building site – earth, lime, stone, plants – are the most pleasant to see and touch, and we need not burn much coal, oil or nuclear fuel when we convert them for use and carry them to the site. The roof and walls will not poison us, and when the building comes to the end of its life it will crumble into earth to support the life of future generations.
>
> (Lea 1994: 40)

Life cycle sustainability assessment

If we wish to assess the sustainability of a building in the objective world, all of its relevant life cycle implications must be considered. A sustainability analysis of all the life cycle phases we will term a Life cycle Sustainability Evaluation (LSE). While several well-known assessment techniques have been developed to evaluate aspects of sustainability, none by itself offers a complete analysis.

Generally the assessments focus on the environment and the economic subsystems.

Environment assessment

Two basic methodological frameworks have been developed for environmental assessment: Environmental Impact Assessment (EIA) and Life Cycle Assessment (LCA). As Crawley and Aho (1999) observe, 'most of the currently applied building environmental assessment methods are in a sense crossbreeds of the two approaches'. Although in principle they share the aim of objectively identifying and assessing the environmental impacts of their study targets, they differ in one fundamental sense. The EIA process aims to assess the actual environmental impacts of a building (or proposed building) located on a given site and in a given context. The LCA technique, on the other hand, is formulated to assess the non-site-specific potential environmental impacts of a product regardless of where, when or who uses it.

The first step in either methodology is *inventory analysis*. In this step, the life cycle inputs and outputs of the product, process or activity are catalogued and quantified. This includes, for example, fossil fuel consumption, airborne emissions (greenhouse gases – GHGs), waterborne emissions, solid emissions and raw materials. Within these categories, each kind of impact is identified as the exchange of a particular substance with the environment. This 'substance' could be a pollutant like a VOC (volatile organic compound), a waste product, or a raw material like iron ore or an energy source like coal.

The second step is *impact analysis*. Actual data for each identified impact needs to be collected and quantified – but here lies a problem. Preferably actual data for specific products, produced in specific factories, should be used, but generally at the design stage neither the actual product is known (unless tightly specified a builder may choose from a range) nor is specific product data available. Pears (2001), for example, when looking at cement manufacture plants, found a wide variation in energy efficiency, greenhouse output and other environmental impacts. Depending on the plant, the embodied energy varied between 3.3 and 8 GJ/tonne. Utilizing region- or country-specific average or generic data in a LCA means that the results are applicable only to that region and not particularly useful for design decision-making outside that region.

The next step is *impact assessment*, quantifying the potential contribution of a product or process to adverse environmental effects. This may involve direct use of all inventory flows, which in effect gives the same weight to all inventory flows. While this may be useful in some cases, giving equal weighting to all impacts is unrealistic. Numbers of approaches have been suggested to combine inventory flows. The US Environment Protection Agency's *Framework for Responsible Environmental Decision-Making* (FRED) introduced 'a decision making framework for achieving a balance among price, technical performance, and environmental preferability' (EPA 2000). In this framework inventory flows are related to ten environmental impacts – global warming potential, acidification potential, eutrophication potential, natural resource depletion, indoor air quality, solid waste, smog, ecological toxicity, human toxicity and ozone depletion. While examining the individual impacts separately may give some idea of a product's performance, the overall performance can only be appreciated when we know the relative importance of each of the potential adverse environmental effects. This involves applying a weighting to each impact and combining them together into a single index of performance.

Economic assessment

Economic performance is generally assessed using the technique of life cycle costing (LCC). LCC attempts to quantify what most designers have generally taken into account implicitly in their selection of design concepts, components and materials, that is, a balance between initial costs and reliability, serviceability and maintenance as reflected in the ongoing costs. The technique of LCC analysis considers total relevant costs over the life of a building (or product in a building) which occur at different times, including costs of acquisition, maintenance, operation and where applicable disposal, and expresses these as equivalent costs at a common time. A major use in designing is to provide information when comparing alternative proposals, for example, an electric hot water system and a solar hot water system.

The principal steps in performing LCC analysis are to specify objectives and constraints applicable to the problem, identify various alternative solutions to be investigated, identify relevant cost items for each option, determine the amounts and timing of the relevant cash flows, and finally calculate the life cycle costs using a discounting technique. The building as a whole may be the subject of an economic assessment to determine overall feasibility or subsystems within the building system may be isolated for economic assessment. For example, the life cycle cost related to the thermal subsystem of a building may be considered by calculating the present worth of all relevant costs C_T such that:

$$C_T = B + P + E \times \frac{(1 + i)^n - 1}{i(1 + i)^n} + \sum M_i \times P_i + \sum R_i \times P'_i$$

where C_T total present value of costs
        B initial costs of building
        P initial costs of plant (heating and cooling equipment)
        E annual energy costs for heating and cooling
        i appropriate discount rate
        n assumed period for life cycle calculation (life of asset)
        M_i annual maintenance costs for plant and relevant building items
        R_i replacement costs for plant and relevant building items
        P_i appropriate present value factors for uniform series payments
        P'_i appropriate present value factors for one-off payments.

The alternative that provides the minimum C_T is taken as the 'best' in terms of life cycle cost – but LCC can rarely be the sole decision criterion. We must realize that in the selection of any alternative, issues such as the relative initial cost differences between alternatives, the risk of future unforeseen price movements, things not considered, and non-quantifiable benefits and costs, as well as aesthetic and moral considerations, also influence the final decision. The economic assessment does, however, allow one aspect of the trade-off between alternatives to be considered more explicitly than it would otherwise be.

The environmental assessment of building

At the beginning of the computer revolution in the early 1970s, Odum saw 'the building of electronic systems models' as a possible way of bringing together 'well-understood parts to comprehend the group phenomena' (Odum 1970: 11). Numbers of computer models of varying intricacy have been developed with the aim of simulating the complex environmental behaviour of buildings.[9] While many building performance assessment programs deal with a single criterion such as energy use, a number of programs (or schemes) exist that attempt to combine various factors, using inputs from a variety of sources, into a single measure of performance.[10]

The BREEAM (Building Research Establishment Environmental Assessment Method) scheme, first introduced in the UK in 1990, is an example of this approach. BREEAM is a voluntary environmental assessment scheme intended to encourage building owners and operators to adopt green practices, and is employed on an estimated 30 per cent of new office buildings in the UK. It provides a tool and authoritative assessment procedures for quantitative evaluation of the environmental impacts of a building. The evaluation covers nine broad issues including health and comfort, energy, transport, water consumption, materials, land use, site ecology and pollution. Credit points are accumulated against the various performance requirements and finally combined by a weighting method into a final rating. The result is presented on a scale to define Pass, Good, Very Good and Excellent performance.

An international initiative to investigate the development of a comprehensive building environmental assessment was a project titled Green Building Challenge '98, led by Natural Resources Canada. The overall goal of GBC '98 was to 'develop, test, and demonstrate an improved method of measuring building performance'. The project reconciled earlier assessment work around the world and a so-called 'second-generation' framework for assessing energy and environmental performance was developed during the process. The method was implemented as a computer tool (GBTool) that provides a framework for scoring and weighting parameters, using data that is generated in appropriate computer simulation programs or from other sources of data (Larsson and Cole 1998). In 2001 a new organization, the International Initiative on a Sustainable Built Environment (IISBE) took over the international management and development of the GBTool. Its aim is to enable regional-specific building assessments related to benchmarks based on standards or typical building practices in each participating country. It is not a simulation package and therefore users must use other software tools to simulate energy performance, estimate embodied energy and emissions, predict thermal comfort and air quality, etc. Once data is entered four performance factors are assessed and scored – resource consumption, environmental loading, indoor environmental quality, and quality of service. Two further factors, economics and pre-operations management, are reported without being scored (Cole and Larsson 2000). GBTool may be used to assess predicted or 'potential' performance of an office, multi-unit residential and school buildings at the design stages.

The Eco-Quantum packages developed in The Netherlands are also intended to assist a designer 'to quickly identify environmental consequences of material choices and water and energy consumption of their designs' (Kortman *et al.* 1998). The approach used in this program estimates the environmental performance of a proposed building on the basis of a LCA technique, incorporating eleven environmental factors – an approach similar to the US EPA approach discussed above. In addition four environmental indicators related to the Dutch construction industry – raw material depletion, emissions, energy consumption and waste – are calculated and the total environmental performance evaluated with respect to subjective weightings.

While each of these assessment tools is useful in its own right, they are constructed to give endorsement to a completed design rather than to assist the designer during the design process. To be really successful as an aid to evaluating the sustainability of design proposals a tool must not only address multiple criteria decision-making, but must also facilitate the designer's iterative approach where initial understandings of the problem and means of addressing it are allowed to evolve.

Iterative multiple criteria decision-making

Inherent in each of the building evaluation schemes above is the performance concept assumption that user 'needs' can be attributed to the various building problem subsystems. By determining the user requirements (and criteria) a priori the performance of a proposed building at the design stage can be evaluated in each of its parts. One problem with this approach is that it is difficult to assign priorities to the various subsystem performances. What if a proposed design achieves zero energy consumption for cooling, but at the expense of a limited amount of discomfort, or a plentiful material is used (e.g. straw bales) at the expense of possible increased maintenance? Evaluation techniques such as the GBTool attempt to address this issue by applying explicit weightings to the various objectives, but the question then is 'Who determines the weightings?' Should they be determined, for example, by the decision-maker's preferences related to the performance objectives, or determined on some 'average' basis? As Coldicutt and Williamson (1995) have pointed out, 'design problems do not come fully pre-defined, but rather need to be explored by an iterative approach in which initial understandings of the problem and means of addressing it are refined'. While some environmental design purists argue that the weighting of objectives is fundamentally wrong because it skews the results and 'the fact that some building types are inherently less sustainable would not become apparent, and there would be no questioning of the status quo' (Vale, Vale and Fay 2001), the reality would seem to be that since most (all) design is done within a context of limited resources, (for example, a limited project budget) the setting of priorities is an inevitable part of design. It is, in fact, the essence of design decision-making. To match this reality a flexible design evaluation methodology should be structured so that neither the objectives to be included nor their assigned weightings are assumed a priori. Because it is rarely possible to determine objective weightings a priori; a designer would probably want to test their sensitivities as part of the design exploration.

Multiple-criteria decision techniques provide a method of dealing with this type of evaluation, related to complex building systems and determining 'best' solutions. Although potentially very complicated, the reduction of all subsystem goals to two sets that we might call costs and benefits simplifies the problem. Figure 5.5 shows the boundary of a set of feasible building solutions with just two objectives (or goals) $Z1$ and $Z2$. So-called Pareto optimal performances are located around a surface where for any $Z1$ the $Z2$ is a maximum. Any solution on this surface may be considered a good solution depending on the method chosen for dealing with trade-offs. Generally, this method is not apparent in that there is no clear or most appropriate way to choose between design solutions that are members of the Pareto optimal set. There are various methods of identifying designs whose performances are members of the Pareto set but with relatively small numbers of cases, the set can be determined directly from identified designs by the enumeration of their performances in the various subsystems defined for the problem.

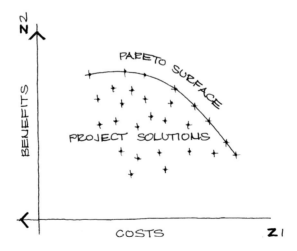

5.5 Pareto optimal surface (drawn by Deborah White).

The convenient way of approaching the multiple-criteria problem is to convert it into a single-criterion problem by forming a weighted sum of the criteria or objective functions for each solution. Radford and Gero (1988) describe this technique as 'Additive Composition' that can be formulated in terms of the familiar cost-benefit analysis model such that the net benefit of a solution A_j is given by,

$$\sum_{k=1}^{p} W_k B_k(A_j) - W_r C_j = [A_j]$$

where

W_k are weights attached to each of p objectives perceived as a benefit $B_k(A_j)$ over j solutions, for example, reduced delivered energy consumption, reduced CO_2 emission etc.

C_j is life cycle cost of solution j, and

W_r expresses the relative weighing associated with the weighted benefits (W_b) and the life cycle cost functions (W_c) for solution j. $W_r = W_c/W_b$

In the design exploration process a set of performances for the various proposed designs are generated, whether or not they lie amongst the Pareto set. Because only a relatively small number of variations would be examined for each project, the Pareto set is identified by inspection on a cost-benefit plot. To provide a consistent method of measurement for the benefit and cost values (so we are not adding or comparing apples and oranges) each objective is best standardized against a reference solution. In this way they become a dimensionless measure of the relative benefit or cost compared with that reference solution. The aim of any sustainable design process can then be conceived in practical terms, as producing a new design incrementally *more sustainable* relative to the reference building. This reference building could be an agreed standard or merely a similar building designed last week (Soebarto and Williamson 2001).

In the same way that user requirements, assessment criteria and objective weightings cannot be determined a priori, there is no a priori method for choosing among the solutions that comprise the Pareto set. Three possible decision methods are:

1   Maximum net benefit, where we seek a solution for which A_j is maximum. This formulation is not sensitive to the classification of a project effect as a cost or a benefit.
2   Best compromise solution, where we seek a solution closest to the best performances for each criteria Z1 and Z2.
3   Maximum benefit-cost ratio, expressed as $\Sigma B/\Sigma C$. This is often advocated in building performance literature as a legitimate decision rule. The ranking of solutions in this case is not insensitive to the allocation of an objective as a benefit or a cost.

Each decision method is likely to give a different 'best' solution so in the general case, context-specific and problem-specific issues will determine which decision criterion is most relevant. If the potential of building environmental assessment programs is to be realized they must be conceived to allow, not only for the uncertainty of the physical affects, but equally the uncertainty inherent in human decision-making. This must allow all assumptions to be recognized.

Recognizing assumptions

Whenever we think about what to do to address some situation, we make assumptions about how problems should be defined. We cannot avoid making some assumptions, as our understandings of reality, as mediated in ways by language, necessarily give us some starting points: we are not blank slates.

Because we need to make assumptions in order to define problems, theory regarding problem-definition is located uncomfortably at the intersection of the open world of practice and the bounded worlds of bodies of theory. This situation is most obvious when the theory is most clearly bounded, as it is in much applied science. Writing about the application of a systems approach to environmental studies, Bennett and Chorley note that:

> A bounded system is one whose operation is entirely justified by its internally specified parts and relationships such that, if inputs occur, the resulting changes within the system and the outputs are capable of exact and unique prediction, given a perfect knowledge of the system.
>
> (Bennett and Chorley 1978: 5)

They go on to say that unbounded systems intersect with others, and are indeterminate. They also suggest that for all observational and experimental scientific work, it is assumed that systems can reasonably be taken as bounded. While these generalizations can be questioned, they are a common approach and are taken as a useful starting point for much decision-making. When theory is applied in the objective world, the dilemma involved in this notion of bounded systems is that theory, being theory, is not the same as the aspects of the objective world that it represents, and so assumptions must always be made about the connections between the theory and the thing, action, feeling or other entity that it represents. For much applied science the need to make assumptions scarcely hinders application, so that we can almost believe that the knowledge gained is 'real'. But this way of thinking gets us into trouble if we try to use it for all application of theory. In addition, it will not suffice for defining real-world problems for the purpose of action. This involves not only the representation, or description of what is, but is also concerned in terms of sustainability with what *ought to be* and the value we place on present or deferred actions. As Baron explains in his book on thinking and deciding '[w]e cannot draw moral conclusions (logically) from facts alone' (Baron 1988: 376).

Notes

1   [H]umans cannot generally be expected to take on the world as a totality. Instead, we engage pieces of it, optimistically anticipating and therefore projecting a more comprehensive structure from these pieces. . . . We need some way to imagine how the world might be put together from pieces whose existence, if they could be revealed, would disclose the many decisions and judgements that support the whole.

(Dripps 1999: 67)

2 See Herman Daly (1999: 52–3) *Ecological Economics and the Ecology of Economics* for a discussion of how the use of essentially non-renewable resources (e.g. metal ores) might be handled in this kind of definition through making provision for the future substitution of 'equivalent' resources.

3 The kind of quantitative modelling that would allow confident statements about environmental impacts is in its infancy, but can still be useful. The validity and usefulness of any quantitative model should be judged

    Not against an imaginary perfection, but in comparison with the mental and descriptive models that we should otherwise use. We should judge (them) by the certainty with which they show the correct time-varying consequences of the statements made by the models compared with the unreliable conclusions we often reach in extending our mental image of system structure to its behavioural implications.

(Forrester 1968)

4 For example, Markus, Whyman *et al.* (1972: 4) propose a conceptual model of the system of buildings and people which has five components:

1   Building system
2   Environmental system
3   Activity system
4   Objectives system
5   Resources system.

This is a descriptive system that uses terms that may also be used for prescription. While, in this particular systems approach, it is noted that 'any designer is free to . . . substitute the employee's, the public's or his own objectives' (Markus, Whyman *et al.* 1972: 6), for the particular objectives described by the authors comprising the objectives system, the approach does not encourage such substitutions.

5   It is fortunate that the metals, which are very energy-intensive in extraction from raw resource, are also the most easily recycled. . . . At present the total effect of recycling on most construction resources is small, for two reasons. Firstly, in the present circumstances of continuing growth, the availability of recycled feedstock is low. Secondly, not all materials and products are suitable for recycling. However . . . [t]he design life of typical buildings being constructed now will extend well into the anticipated crisis period [in the availability of some resources]. It is clear that lifespan factor and recycling potential should be taken into account in current design thinking.

(Fawcett and Lim 1998)

6 There are many instances of rebuilding after war and natural disaster where reconstructing the previously existing form and character of development has been seen to

be a key part of maintaining a sense of belonging and cultural continuity. In urban design, the 'new urbanism' movement draws on and promotes this sense of continuity. Well-known examples of the new urbanism that take forms derived at least in part from local vernaculars include Seaside in Florida, US, and Poundbury in Dorset, UK.

7 There have been expressions of concern over gases emitted by some building materials in insufficiently ventilated buildings, as well as air pollution resulting from the use of buildings.

8 This is the approach adopted in the automobile industry, with the separation and labelling of different plastics and metals for easier recycling.

9 The USD Department of Environment web site http://www.eren.doe.gov/buildings/ tools directory/ lists more than 200 energy tools and computer packages.

10 Some of the computer tools available to assess sustainability aspects of design decisions in various countries are: US – LEED, BEES, Green Building Advisor, France – COMFIE, PAPOOSE, EQUER, Canada – ATHENA, The Netherlands – ECO-it, Australia – EnerRate.

6 Green houses

We have highlighted the cultural construction of sustainability, drawn attention to a variety of ethical positions, explored the nature of decision-making and design advice, and discussed the complex systems involved, but how do all these come together when we as architects are faced with making day-to-day designs? To illustrate the complexity of the problem we as architects face in terms of the social, scientific and professional positions, we consider in this chapter just one issue – the design of houses in relation to the risk of climate change. At the start of the twenty-first century climate change (and associated global warming) is often framed as the single dominant concern for sustainable building design. To understand how such a theme has emerged in the discourse we must look at the larger institutional settings of global science and global politics. To appreciate how architects have responded to this theme, we can begin by looking at some of the history of associations between climate and architecture.

Climate and architecture

The idea that the climate should shape approaches to building design is not new and is a well-accepted part of architectural discourse. As far back as the first century AD Vitruvius, when giving advice on the design of houses in the far-flung regions of the Roman Empire, says that the climate should determine the style of house:

> If our designs for private houses are to be correct, we must at the outset take note of the countries and climates in which they are built. One style of house seems appropriate to build in Egypt, another in Spain, a different kind in Pontus, one still different in Rome, . . . because one part of the earth is directly under the sun's course, another is far away from it . . . hence, as the position of the heaven with regard to a given tract on the earth leads naturally to different characteristics . . . it is obvious that designs for houses ought similarly to conform to the nature of the country and to diversities of climate.
> (Vitruvius 1960: 170)

While climate and building design intersect in the discourse, the reason and the function of the union has shown subtle shifts over time. A review of recent

6.1 A 'solar efficient' house: Norton Summit house, architects Energy Architecture, designed with solar oriented glass, thermal mass, solar power, solar hot water and self-contained sewage system (photographer Terry Williamson).

climate/building connections is instructive in positioning the present debate as it shows that as the function shifts elements of the discourse are carried along, sometimes modified, always adding to the richness of the discourse, but also providing the possibility of introducing ignorance with errors in defining or interpreting the design problem.

In 1915 the American geographer Ellsworth Huntington (Huntington 1915) proposed a theory that climate was integrally connected to the rise of civilizations. This theme was taken up by several writers in the 1940s, such as Clarence Mills (Professor of Experimental Medicine at the University of Cincinnati) in his book *Climate Makes the Man* (Mills 1946) and Sydney Markham (one time Parliamentary Secretary to the English Prime Minister, Ramsay MacDonald) in *Climate and the Energy of Nations* (Markham 1944). Mills explained the nature and consequences of a good climate and Markham connects this to climate control in buildings.

Temperate-zone nations are leaders in world affairs. Their people, activated by cool climates, have had the energy to build great power plants, sky-scrapers, dams, bridges, and a legion of impressive monuments to human initiative. They visit the tropics mainly for trade and war, and have long benefited from tropical raw material wealth which the natives are too sluggish to exploit. . . .

(Mills 1946: 44)

I am convinced that one of the basic reasons for the rise of a nation in modern times is its control over climatical conditions. . . . Civilisation to a great degree depends upon climate control in a good natural climate.

(Markham 1944: 20)

And further,

Where indoor temperatures are above 60°F and below 76°F, and the relat-ive humidities between 40 per cent and 70 per cent, men work harder and more efficiently than at temperatures and humidities outside this zone.

(Markham 1944: 31)

Referring to developments in the Prairie Provinces of Canada and Queensland in Australia, Markham says that the great progress (prior to 1947) had been achieved because immigrants brought their energies with them: 'for a time [the progress in] these areas are bound to reflect these energies . . . But sooner or later climate will tell' (Markham 1944: 209). He then goes on to suggest that if Queensland is to continue its progress, climate control must be acquired, as acclimatization to hot and humid weather has resulted in a gradually lowering working efficiency. Mills, however, questioned the use of air conditioning on a large scale saying:

The difference [between heating and cooling] lies in the fact that winter heating is essential while summer cooling is more or less a luxury. Hot-weather comfort is particularly costly in tropical climates, where the cool-ing load is heavy and electricity rates are high. . . .While proper conditioning of man's indoor habitat may add greatly to his comfort and health, it is questionable whether it can go far toward overcoming the more profound effects of given climates upon whole masses of people.

(Mills 1946: 123)

While today we see these views as vestiges of imperial ideology and rather silly, at the time undertones of these notions are to be found even in 'official' publications. A UK Heating and Ventilation Committee of the Department of Scientific and Industrial Research (Heating and Ventilation [Reconstruction] Committee, 1945) examined requirements for the heating and ventilation of

UK houses. While stating that their recommendations were based on basic human needs for warmth, their report cautioned that: 'It is possible to have too much comfort, for the body may then lose its power of quick adaptation, which is an essential requirement for normal health' (Heating and Ventilation [Reconstruction] Committee 1945: 13).

In 1949 the Australian Government's Commonwealth Experimental Building Station (CEBS) released the first in a series called the *Notes on the Science of Building*. Over more than twenty years, these *Notes* became a substantial and authoritive set of design advice documents. The first note was titled *Design for Climate* and discusses the design of domestic buildings for the hot arid and hot humid climates of Australia. The introductory paragraph echoes almost exactly the sentiments of Mills and Markham, where climate and the building design as the object of discourse is linked to the function of maintaining the 'energies of white people'. 'The loss of energy and efficiency experienced by white people in hot climates is difficult to assess, but it is appreciable, and justifies considerable attention to the improvement of physical conditions of both working and living' (CEBS 1949).

In more recent times the connection between climate and building design is proclaimed in the titles of the classical texts on building thermal performance design.[1] As van Straaten reveals, writing in the late 1960s, the function of the climate/architecture discourse shifts to providing an acceptable thermal environment:

> People are no longer satisfied with dull and dingy interiors but demand ample lighting, visually pleasant surroundings, low noise levels, adequate ventilation and acceptable thermal conditions. This applies not only to countries with a highly developed economy but also to developing countries where large masses still live in comparative poverty.
>
> (van Straaten 1967: v)

By the mid-1970s the connection between climate and building design had changed from the issue of providing adequate thermal conditions for working and living to the function of promoting energy efficiency and reducing the fuel energy required to meet specified comfort conditions. It was around this time that in many countries regulation of aspects of the thermal performance of buildings (especially dwellings) was introduced. The present day focus of the climate and building design discourse has again changed and is now centrally concerned, at least at the political level, with the issue of averting possible climate changes by cutting greenhouse gases (GHG) emissions.

Since how we position ourselves as architects with respect to the issue of climate change revolves around an understanding of the science of global warming, we give a brief introduction to this subject. Here the system of interest is the whole of our planet and its atmosphere. The input to the system is solar energy and the output is heat loss to surrounding space. The variables within the system are numerous and their relationships complex; we see that a part of the problem is just what variables are important and how we understand the way the system behaves.

The science of global warming

The composition of the Earth's atmosphere is a principal factor in establishing the planet's temperature, and this in turn sets the conditions for all life on Earth. Without the heat-trapping properties of so-called 'greenhouse gases', which make up only a small fraction of the Earth's atmosphere, the average surface temperature of the Earth would be like that of Mars, that is around minus 16°C.

Greenhouse gases are those gases that are transparent to solar radiation but opaque to longwave radiation. Their action is similar to that of glass in a greenhouse. The main greenhouse gases are water vapour (H_2O), carbon dioxide (CO_2), methane (CH_4), nitrous oxide (N_2O), and halocarbons (such as CFC-11 and CFC-12). With the exception of halocarbons, most greenhouse gases occur naturally. Water vapour is by far the most common, with an atmospheric concentration of nearly 1 per cent, compared with less than 0.04 per cent for carbon dioxide. Concentrations of other greenhouse gases are a fraction of that for carbon dioxide.

Increasing concentrations

Scientists had reported increasing concentrations of carbon dioxide in the atmosphere for most of this century, but permanent and reliable monitoring stations were established only in the 1950s. Concentrations of methane and nitrous oxide have been recorded since the mid-1980s and all measurements have recorded increasing atmospheric concentrations of these greenhouse gases.

In addition, since the initial discovery that carbon dioxide concentrations in the atmosphere were increasing, scientists have exercised ingenuity in pushing the record of atmospheric concentrations backward in time, using samples of 'fossil air' trapped in ice cores from Greenland and the Antarctic. These long-run records appear to indicate that the carbon dioxide concentrations in the Earth's atmosphere stand at levels not previously attained (at least for any prolonged period) over the past 420,000 years (IPCC 2001a: Section C.1). Table 6.1 shows the increased concentrations of several main greenhouse gases from the pre-industrial period. All observations suggest that the growth in concentrations has occurred largely in the past 200 years, and especially since 1940. The timing of the growth in concentrations, together with anomalous variations in observations between the northern and southern hemispheres, implies that the prime source for the growth in CO_2 concentrations is the combustion of fossil fuels, particularly in the northern hemisphere's industrialized countries.

Although the increasing concentrations of atmospheric greenhouse gases are an indisputable fact, its significance and effects remained a matter of some speculation among atmospheric scientists and climatologists during the 1960s

Table 6.1 Global atmospheric concentrations of greenhouse gases

Item	Atmospheric CO_2 [(ppm)]	Atmospheric methane [(ppb)]	Atmospheric nitrous oxide [(ppb)]	CFC-11 [(ppt)]	HFC-23 [(ppt)]
Pre-industrial concentration	280	700	270	0	0
Concentration in 1998	365	1745	314	267	14
Trend per year, 1990s	1.5	7.0	0.8	−1.4	0.55

Source: IPCC (2001a), Table 4.1(a).

Notes: ppm   parts per million (10^6)
       ppb   parts per billion (10^9)
       ppt   parts per trillion (10^{12})

and 1970s. Many believed at that time that the net effect of industrial and agricultural atmospheric emissions would result in a general cooling of the earth's atmosphere. By the mid-1980s, scientific assessments began to assert that CO_2 and other greenhouse gases could contribute to global warming. However, this view is still not without its challengers who argue that scientific proof is incomplete or contradictory, and that there remain many uncertainties about the nature and cause of the Earth's climate.

In 1988 the World Meteorological Organization and the United Nations Environment Programme established an Intergovernmental Panel on Climate Change (IPCC) to examine available scientific research on climate change and to provide scientific advice to policymakers. Their work examined the science of global warming together with the implications of possible warming on such factors as sea level rise, precipitation levels, surface temperature, mid-latitude continental dryness (droughts), response of ecosystems and the incidence of severe storms. Their first assessment of climate change report was released in 1990 (IPCC 1990) and provided the scientific and technical base for the *UN Framework Convention on Climate Change* (UNFCCC 1992). A second assessment report followed in 1995 (IPCC 1995) and a third in 2001 (IPCC 2001b).

The central body of work reported by the IPCC involves complex climate modelling by computer simulation. These models show that there is a causal relationship between atmospheric GHG concentrations and average global temperature. Increases in GHGs cause the temperature of the earth to increase. The earlier simulations showed that if atmospheric greenhouse gas concentrations continued to increase, by the year 2100 the earth would heat up by 8°C. The latest global climate computer models, using a variety of input variable scenarios, predict smaller rises in the range 1.4–5.8°C warming over the period 1990 to 2100 (IPCC 2001a: Chapter 9). It is hypothesized that these temperature increases could lead to changes in the weather and in the level of the oceans around the world. In turn, these changes may prove disruptive to current patterns of land use and human settlement, as well as to existing ecosystems.

Many point to recent apparently extreme weather conditions around the world as being indicative of long-term climate change.

Data from land temperature measurements at meteorological stations and sea surface temperatures seem to support the models, as they purported to show a temperature increase around the earth of $0.6 \pm 0.2°C$ over this century with most of this increase occurring in two periods 1910–1945 and 1976–2000 (IPCC 2001a: section 2.2.2.3).

The computer programs that predict that the global surface temperature will increase also predict that the troposphere temperature would increase as fast or faster (Lomborg 2001: 269). Measurements taken over the last twenty years or so using weather balloons and satellite technology, however, show little change over this period. Some scientists argue that the surface temperature measurements are in error for several reasons, the principal one being the heat island effect in populated areas.

Research by building scientists looking into the possible influence of the heat island effect on air conditioning energy consumption would seem to add some weight to this contention. Santamouris *et al.* (2001) assessed the climate variability in and around Athens, Greece at thirty urban and suburban sites. They found the average daily heat island intensity (the temperature compared with a rural site) for urban sites to be approximately $10°C$ with a maximum value of around $15°C$. A study in Adelaide, Australia found that city sites could be up to $10°C$ hotter at night compared with temperatures in the surrounding parklands no more than 2 kilometres away (Williamson and Erell 2001). While this heat increase may be associated with human influence (the construction of urban forms, changes in vegetation, heat release into the atmosphere) the effects are confined to, and explained by, effects within the level of the urban boundary layer. If as Bjørn Lomborg explains, 'it is true that the temperature has increased, although mainly at night, in the winter, and in cold places' (Lomborg 2001: 299) then the observations may be explained without resort to the greenhouse effect.

There are many complexities in estimating the likelihood of global warming; sceptics question many of the findings of the IPCC and call into question the reliability of the computer climate models used to make projections of future warming. Even the latest IPCC report acknowledges certain inadequacies of the models in that they:

> Cannot yet simulate all aspects of climate (e.g., they still cannot account fully for the observed trend in the surface–troposphere temperature difference since 1979) and there are particular uncertainties associated with clouds and their interaction with radiation and aerosols.
>
> (IPCC 2001a: 9)

In recommending action be taken by the nations of the world to curb greenhouse gas emissions, the IPCC 1995 report was somewhat guarded in its conclusions.

Our ability to quantify the human influence on global climate is currently limited because the expected signal is still emerging from the noise of natural variability, and because there are uncertainties in key factors. These include the magnitude and patterns of long-term natural variability and the time-evolving pattern of forcing by, and response to, changes in concentrations of greenhouse gases and aerosols, and land surface changes. Nevertheless, the balance of evidence suggests that there is a discernible human influence on global climate.

(IPCC 1995)

Six years on, the IPCC 2001 report is less circumspect in its findings and says with confidence, 'There is new and stronger evidence that most of the warming observed over the last 50 years is attributable to human activities' (IPCC 2001b).

There are scientists who hotly dispute this finding, arguing that solar activity has a much more dominating effect on climate than assumed in the existing climate models and therefore the anthropogenic influence on climate is not as potent as assumed in the IPCC reports. The work of Theodor Landscheidt in providing successful long range forecasting of climate events such as El Niño, based exclusively on sunspot activity, adds weight to this view (Landscheidt 2002). Nevertheless global warming and global politics have become intertwined and we shall consider this issue next. We begin by looking at this question from a global perspective and will work our way down to a more local level.

The international politics

By the mid-1980s, the global warming issue entered the arena of global politics. Paterson (1996) gives an account of negotiations leading up to the framing of the *UN Convention on Climate Change* (UNFCCC 1992). In late 1990, and following a resolution of the Second World Climate Change Conference that had the first IPCC report available for consideration, the UN established the Intergovernmental Negotiation Committee (INC) to draft a *Framework Convention on Climate Change*. In what some saw as pre-emptive moves to counter possible measures that were more severe, many of the industrialized countries had by 1990 already put in place unilateral undertakings ostensibly aimed at reducing greenhouse gas emissions.

After considerable negotiation the Convention was submitted for signature at the Earth Summit in Rio de Janeiro in June, 1992. The main objective of the UNFCCC is to:

Achieve . . . stabilization of the greenhouse gas concentrations in the atmosphere at a level that would prevent dangerous anthropogenic interference with the climate system. Such a level should be achieved within a timeframe sufficient to allow ecosystems to adapt naturally to climate change, to ensure that food production is not threatened and to enable economic development to proceed in a sustainable manner.

(United Nations 1992a: Article 2)

As a framework treaty, the Convention set out principles and general commitments but left more specific obligations to later negotiations. The Convention itself relies on voluntary commitments by the signature countries to take steps to satisfy its objectives. In its implementation the Convention distinguishes between developed countries (Annex I countries) and developing countries ('non-Annex I countries'). General commitments under the Convention, which apply to both developed and developing countries, are to adopt national programmes for mitigating climate change; to develop adaptation strategies; to promote the sustainable management and conservation of greenhouse gas 'sinks' (such as forests); to take climate change into account when setting relevant social, economic, and environmental policies; to cooperate in technical, scientific, and educational matters and to promote scientific research and the exchange of information.

The Convention requires Annex I countries to take the strongest measures, although the states in transition to a market economy (essentially the ex-Soviet Union countries) are allowed certain flexibility. It recognizes that compliance by developing countries will depend on financial and technical assistance from developed countries. The needs of the least developed countries and those that are particularly vulnerable to the possible climate change for geographical reasons are given special attention. Annex I countries were to limit emissions of carbon dioxide and other greenhouse gases, with the aim of returning to 1990 emissions levels by the year 2000. The Convention permitted several states to join together to adopt a common emission reduction target. The developed countries are required to facilitate the transfer of technology and provide financial resources to developing countries to help them implement the Convention. Also, the Convention requires developed countries to finance the costs incurred by developing countries for submitting reports on their greenhouse gas emissions and measures for implementing the treaty. This financial assistance is to be 'new and additional', rather than redirected from existing development aid funds. Shortly after ratification of the Convention in December 1993, it became apparent that countries such as the United States and Japan would not meet the voluntary stabilization targets by 2000. A number of other important questions were also raised in the international arena:

- How can the international community strike the necessary balance between expanding the pace of economic development and resultant higher energy use and responding adequately to concerns about climate change? It became apparent that measures to reduce the possible threat of global warming (as distinct from global warming itself) must be viewed as an economic problem with serious worldwide implications.
- How can nations gradually but substantially reduce their emissions of greenhouse gases without stalling their economies? and
- How can the burden of protecting the climate be shared most equitably among nations?

The first meeting of the Conference of Parties (COP1) to the UNFCCC was held in Berlin in 1995. Here the *Berlin Mandate*, which established a process to enable governments in developed countries to reduce greenhouse gas emissions in the period beyond 2000, was adopted. The Mandate set out specific policies and measures, taking into account differences in starting points, economic structures, and resource bases among different countries. It also specified that work should be completed as early as possible, so that the objective to reduce emissions of carbon dioxide and other greenhouse gases beginning in 2000 could be adopted at COP3 in Kyoto, scheduled for late 1997. At that meeting, it was hoped to agree on legally binding emission targets.

Leading up to and during the Kyoto Conference there was wide disparity among key players, especially on three items:

- The amount of binding reductions in greenhouse gases to be required, and which gases were to be included in the requirements,
- Whether developing countries should be part of the requirements for greenhouse gas limitations, and
- Whether to allow emissions trading and joint implementation that would give credit for emissions reductions to a country that brings about the actual reductions in another country.

The difficulty of the negotiations is illustrated by the positions adopted by various major stakeholders. The United States, the country with the largest emissions, opposed the setting of quantified targets but proposed that all six major greenhouse gases be reduced to 1990 levels by the period 2008–2012, with joint implementation allowed. The European Union (EU) argued strongly for a 15 per cent reduction from 1990 levels by 2010 for three greenhouse gases, using a joint approach for the nations within the EU, but no joint implementation beyond that. Japan proposed a 5 per cent reduction from 1990 levels for three greenhouse gases. Australia was among a number of countries that argued that differentiated targets should be applied to individual countries and that there should be individual levels for every country, considering its specific situation. They suggested that projected population growth, GDP per capita, emission intensity of GDP, energy intensity of exports, etc., should be factors that determine the greenhouse gas emission limitation or reduction commitment. The group of developing countries (known as the G77 plus China) proposed that the Annex I countries should stabilize their emissions of greenhouse gases at 1990 levels by 2000, then reduce them by 15 per cent by 2010, with further reductions of 20 per cent for a total of 35 per cent reduction below 1990 levels by 2020. The G77 continued to maintain that developing countries should not have greenhouse gas emissions capped, as this would adversely affect their rate of economic progress.

In December 1997, the nations came together to address these questions and to complete negotiations of the *Kyoto Protocol* which, as a follow-on to the original climate treaty, marked the first international attempt to place legally binding limits on greenhouse gas emissions. As determined under the *Kyoto Protocol*, the countries listed in Annex I of the Convention shall:

Individually or jointly, ensure that their aggregate anthropogenic carbon dioxide equivalent emissions of the greenhouse gases do not exceed their assigned amounts, calculated pursuant to their quantified emission limitation and reduction commitments. . . in the commitment period 2008 to 2012.

(United Nations 1997: Article 3)

In addition to CO_2, the primary greenhouse gas, the Protocol focuses on five other greenhouse gases: methane (CH_4), nitrous oxide (N_2O), hydrofluorocarbons (HFCs), perfluorocarbons (PFCs), and sulfur hexafluoride (SF6). Specifically, the Protocol aims to cut the combined emissions of greenhouse gases from developed countries by roughly 5 per cent from their 1990 levels by the 2008– 2012 time frame. It specifies the amount each industrialized nation must contribute toward meeting that reduction goal. The nations with the highest CO_2 emissions – the United States and Japan – were expected to reduce their output by 7 per cent and 6 per cent respectively. The fifteen European Union countries overall are expected to achieve an 8 per cent reduction.[2]

Unlike the Montreal Protocol concerning *Substances That Deplete the Ozone Layer*, which will eventually 'solve' the problem of ozone depletion if adhered to, the *Kyoto Protocol* will not 'solve' the problem of climate change. At best, the *Kyoto Protocol* will only begin the long process of weaning the world away from heavy reliance on fossil fuels, point to the need to change industrial and agricultural practices that produce GHGs and slow down the destruction of forests that act as CO_2 sinks.

Under the Protocol, countries are expected to have made demonstrable progress in achieving their commitments by 2005. Countries in transition to a market economy are allowed some flexibility in achieving their targets. All countries must take steps to formulate national and regional programmes to improve local emissions of greenhouse gas emissions and sinks that remove these gases from the atmosphere. In addition, all countries are committed to formulate, publish, and update climate change mitigation and adaptation measures, and to cooperate in promotion and transfer of environmentally sound technologies and in scientific and technical research on the climate system.

As well as setting down emission commitments for UNFCCC Annex I countries, the *Kyoto Protocol* establishes certain 'flexible mechanisms' that may be used in reaching emission targets. These mechanisms are:

1   Joint implementation among Annex I parties;
2   The Clean Development Mechanism (CDM), which permits investors to earn 'certified emission reduction' units for emission reduction projects in non-Annex I countries, and
3   Trading of emission reduction units among Annex I countries.

No details for the implementation of these mechanisms were established at Kyoto. The rules for implementation were intended to be resolved at the follow-up meeting in Buenos Aires held in November 1998. At this meeting, however, there were deep divisions, particularly between developed and developing countries, and the most that could be achieved was a procedural decision to establish a work programme, known as the *Buenos Aires Plan of Action* (BAPA) for addressing the numerous unresolved issues.

The *Kyoto Protocol* was opened for signature on 16 March, 1998, for one year, but will only enter into force when fifty-five nations have ratified it, provided that these ratifications include Annex I countries that account for at least 55 per cent of total greenhouse gas emissions in 1990. There are no obligations under the Protocol until it enters into force. By 1999, seventy-one countries had signed the treaty, including the United States, the European Union and most of its members, Australia, Canada, Japan, China and a range of developing countries, but only a few small island states had ratified it. While signing the Protocol the US Administration indicated that until developing countries showed commitments to 'meaningful participation' in greenhouse gas limitations, it would not submit the legislation to the Senate for consent. The developing countries for their part argue that the developed countries, being the largest polluters, should bear the major responsibility for emission reductions, and in addition should assist the less developed States with aid programmes and technology transfers so they can establish 'clean' industries.

Follow-up talks in The Hague in 2000 failed to reach agreement. Shortly before a reconvened meeting in Bonn the following year, the United States described the Protocol as 'fatally flawed' and announced that it would withdraw from the Protocol. The meeting went ahead, and after all-night sessions the world community of 186 nations, with the exception of the United States, adopted a 'political agreement' outlining core elements of the *Kyoto Protocol* on 25 July 2001. Draft decisions on several key issues relating to compliance and Land Use, Land-Use Change and Forestry (LULUCF) were referred to COP7. Although concessions made in the Bonn Agreements to the most reluctant signatories meant that the cuts in greenhouse gas emissions by thirty of the world's richest nations would be reduced from Kyoto's 5.2 per cent cut from 1990 levels to only a marginal 1–3 per cent, the New Zealand representative was reported as saying that 'we have delivered probably the most comprehensive and difficult agreement in human history' (Hodgson 2001). The agreement allowed new targets to be set for periods beyond 2010. It also set the framework for an 'international carbon market' by which companies or countries who reduce greenhouse gases beyond the targets would sell their unused pollution rights, a bizarre but perhaps effective incentive to help save the world. Other key components of the agreement were additional funding provided by the industrialized to the developing world to help it adopt clean technologies, and allowing industrialized countries to plant and manage forests and change farming practices as credits towards removing carbon dioxide from the atmosphere.

In November 2001 the Climate Change caravan moved to Marrakesh, Morocco for COP7 with pressure being exerted to conclude a deal so that the Protocol could be ratified in time for the Johannesburg Summit (Rio + 10 Earth Summit 2) in September 2002. Despite the general optimism over the Bonn

Agreements, many technical issues still remained to be solved and the umbrella group of countries both collectively and individually (notably Australia, the Russian Federation, Japan and Canada) continued to demonstrate a remarkable degree of intransigence on many details. On 10 November 2001 consensus on all aspects of the BAPA were finally achieved, thus paving the way for ratification and entering into force of the Protocol. Since that date the US Administration declared a unilateral programme to reduce greenhouse gas emissions. In announcing the initiative President Bush said:

> I'm confident that the environmental path that I announce will benefit the entire world. This new approach is based on this common-sense idea: that economic growth is key to environmental progress, because it is growth that provides the resources for investment in clean technologies. This new approach will harness the power of markets, the creativity of entrepreneurs, and draw upon the best scientific research.
>
> (Bush 2002)

Australia too appears to have all but abandoned the Protocol, and has joined the US government in a Climate Action Partnership to focus on 'practical' approaches to dealing with climate change.[3]

This has presented a picture of the political context up to 2002, as an illustration of the way that international competitiveness and self-interest interact with shared concerns and determination in addressing a perceived global problem.[4] We will now turn to consider how buildings and their design are implicated in climate change issues.

Global warming and building design

If we examine the national communications submitted to the United Nations under Article 12 of the *United Nations Framework Convention on Climate Change* (1997) we see that many include references to aspects of building design and operation as measures introduced or proposed for introduction to reduce GHG emissions. Many countries attribute GHG emissions from buildings to be in the range 20–30 per cent of their total national emissions.

The range of policy tools announced in the communications includes fuel substitutions, economic instruments (including pricing, taxation and market-based incentives schemes), regulatory measures and/or voluntary programmes (including energy audits, appliance labelling and building certification) and public education and information programmes. Almost without exception, the rhetoric is couched in terms of energy requirements (savings, conservation, management or energy efficiency), despite the fact that many economists now view as simplistic, the article of faith held by many, that the promotion of energy efficiency at the micro level will reduce energy consumption at the macro level (Herring 1999). The measures proposed in the national responses often have a direct impact on the design of buildings. Many of the advisory and incentive schemes that have been introduced in a variety of countries incorporate building design advice that is aimed at improving the energy efficiency of buildings – both residential and commercial. In many cases mandatory envelope thermal insulation requirements for residential and commercial buildings, first introduced in many countries in the time following the 1970s oil shocks, have been strengthened. A variety of energy codes and green building design schemes have been introduced that have as a primary aim the reduction of energy use (and greenhouse gas emissions). Claims are routinely made that for many existing and proposed buildings these programmes can produce energy savings in the range of 35–50 per cent. Many countries admit however that in reality, in both the residential and commercial sectors, energy efficiency improvements at best act simply to offset the growth in the number, size and improved standards of buildings. For example, the communication from Greece says:

> Regarding the *domestic and tertiary sector*, the improving standards of living resulted in higher levels of heating and recently of cooling, while the increase in the number of dwelling units resulted in a rise in the ownership of home electric appliances. Energy demand for ventilation, lighting and other office equipment in the tertiary sector has also increased. However, there is a number of factors helping to reduce the rate of increase in energy consumption (e.g. installation of thermal insulation in private residences and apartment buildings, installation of solar water heating units in residences and hotels, the installation of double glazing in new and in some cases in older buildings, replacement or modernization of older electric and heating appliances etc.).
>
> (Greece 1997)

Studies in other countries also show that, rather than stabilizing or reducing, GHG emissions due to buildings are increasing at a rapid rate. Reports by the Australian Greenhouse Office conclude that even with the most optimistic scenario, greenhouse gas emissions in 2010 are expected to have risen by 15 per cent above 1990 levels in the residential sector, and by as much as 50 per cent for the commercial sector (AGO 1999).

Building design and climate change

To see the implications of the science and the politics of climate change for producing a sustainable architecture, we need to take a step back and review the information we have. The IPCC climate assessments assert that GHG emissions would appear to be influencing the climate and that unless this process is reversed significant climate change will occur. There are however acknowledged differences in the 'scientific' findings regarding uncertainties of predicting the magnitude, timing, rate, and regional consequences of potential climatic change. There are also sceptics who argue that the anthropogenic influence on climate is overstated. The political arena of climate change is no less ambiguous. The *Kyoto Protocol*, if ratified by the required number of states, will have only a minor influence on the overall GHG emissions. Then we have an ethical dilemma: do the different commitments under the Protocol for Annex I countries and the absence of commitments from non-Annex I countries mean an architect has different obligations depending on where they practice or build? Adding to the confusion is the exaggerated claims of doomsayers who attribute every severe weather event to climate change, when even the most recent IPCC report clearly states that 'small-scale phenomena, such as thunderstorms, tornadoes, hail and lightning', cannot be accounted for in climate models (IPCC 2001a: 15). But the main problem is that the mitigation measures in place or proposed fail in almost every case to take a whole-of-problem approach. If full problem definition is essential to sustainable architecture, then despite the rhetoric we are far from achieving this goal.

Dealing with climate change involves several specific issues that we could expect to be addressed, either explicitly or implicitly, during the design of a building. These include:

- Reducing the GHG emissions that are produced during the manufacture, transport and putting in place of the materials of construction,
- Reducing the GHG emissions from the operation of the building, and
- Responding to the predictable or imagined effects of climate change such as global warming, the higher intensity of rainfall or increased humidity.

Dealing with these issues simultaneously, together with other more general issues such as budgetary constraints or community preferences in a full problem definition, requires maturity in the way the practice and processes of architecture are conceived and relevant ends addressed. This maturity would seem a long way off. When 350 architects in Australia were asked to nominate the 'important factors that define good design' only 30 per cent of responses included issues concerned with impact of buildings on the environment. Function, aesthetics and context rated as the most important factors for good design (Wittmann 1997). When the same architects were asked what sustainable design features they included in their last five designs, a rather narrow conception of the issue was obvious from the responses. The most frequently mentioned features were orientation, shading, insulation and natural ventilation, indicating that the architects conceive sustainability in very limited terms, and more allied to the concept of energy-efficient design rather than a broader range of issues.

Similarly, the advice an architect might get on tackling climate change does not deal with the issue in a holistic way, again despite rhetoric to the contrary. We can illustrate this with two examples, both of which show the importance of carefully defining all the relevant objectives of the design problem.

Clean and safe electricity

Since the primary source of GHG emissions related to buildings is due to the burning of fossil fuels, this issue is of course linked to energy consumption: the electricity, the gas and any other fuels used in the building. The second national communication by France required by the UNFCCC says:

> France's energy policy since the first oil crisis has already permitted a substantial reduction in CO_2 emissions and therefore of France's contribution to the greenhouse effect.
>
> This policy relied in particular on the following items:
>
> - Defining stringent regulations aimed at fostering energy savings. Thermal housing regulations are a prime example.
> - Taxation policy . . .
> - A major energy saving and efficiency awareness program has been implemented . . .
> - The development of a large nuclear industry enables reducing CO_2 emissions, not only in France but in the other Member-States of the European Union.
>
> (République Française 1997: 3)

This last initiative reflects a long-standing policy to promote nuclear power[5] as a safe and clean source of energy. Publicity from Électricité de France (EDF) has actually suggested that this electricity is an eco-product. In an interview with a leading construction industry magazine Christian Sulle, marketing manager for EDF, said:

> L'utilisation de l'énergie électrique n'entraîne par elle-même aucune pollution sur les milieux naturels. Elle possède toutes les caractéristiques d'un écoproduit. (*'The use of electricity does not have any pollution effects of itself on the natural environment. It [electricity] possesses all the characteristics of an eco-product.'*)
>
> (Sulle 1993)

If GHG reduction was the only objective to be considered, then this argument could have some validity. However, electricity generated by nuclear power and promoted as a clean energy source denies the many environmental concerns associated with its use, such as the risk of catastrophic accidents, the possible dangers in transporting both the uranium and the spent fuel, the short and long term pollution, not to mention mining on aboriginal sacred lands and national parks in Australia.[6] Unless these issues are included as part of the problem definition, the problem will be ill-defined and potentially misguided decisions taken.

House energy rating

House or Home Energy Rating Schemes or Systems (HERS) are cited in several UNFCCC National communications as a measure aimed at reducing residential GHG emissions. For the US, Home Energy Rating Systems are referred to in the *US Climate Action Report* (US State Department 1997) as a means of providing finance for incorporating whole building energy-efficient features into house designs. In Australia state and local governments have introduced a Nationwide House Energy Rating Scheme (NatHERS) as a minimum energy performance requirement for new housing and extensions to improve energy efficiency (Commonwealth of Australia 1997). In the United Kingdom, recent amendments to the building regulations require new dwellings and conversions in England and Wales to have a house rating using the Standard Assessment Procedure (SAP) which is the Government's recommended system for home energy rating (UK 1997). This rating is to be displayed in each dwelling. The SAP rating is based on energy costs for space and water heating. The SAP also provides the methodology for calculating a carbon index (CI) related to the CO_2 emissions associated with space and water heating that can be used as one way to comply with the conservation of fuel and power provisions of the building regulations.

So what are HERS? Essentially HERS are a method of rating the energy performance or energy efficiency of a house by calculating (usually incorporating a computer simulation) the energy load and/or energy consumption of a dwelling for several end-uses such as heating, cooling and water heating. Typically a HERS rating is expressed as a number of points, (1–100 or 120), or a number of stars (1–5). A house with a greater number of points or stars is a 'better' house. Inherent in all the methodologies is the assumption of a 'typical' family expressed by occupant-related factors in the calculation such as number of people, number and use of appliances, and thermostat settings. The climate used in the calculations is also standardized. The UK SAP, for example, uses degree-day and solar radiation data that are the average for the UK and cannot account for regional or local weather variations. Apart from the weather issue a house rating has many other potential sources of error such as inaccurate calculation algorithms, incorrect assumptions about the physical properties of the building, wrong assumptions concerning the operation of the building and finally mistakes in data entry to the computer program. The vagaries of the concept are argued away by saying that the HERS expresses the *potential* of the house to be energy efficient.

While HERS claim to use scientific methods aimed at producing energy-efficient dwellings (and that have lower greenhouse gas emissions), this proposition should be tested. A statement about the objective of a HERS would be something like: if you take a house with low HERS points (or stars) and compare it in exactly the same situation to a house with more points (or stars) then the latter will use less energy. This is often explained as taking the same family and moving them from a low rating house to an 'identical' high rating house. If we accept Popper's (Popper 1972) line of demarcation between scientific propositions and statements of pseudo-science or non-science as their 'falsifiability, or refutability, or testability' then the HERS proposition is immediately consigned to the category of non-science. Apart from logistical difficulties of conducting a suitable experiment to test such a statement there is a methodological problem: it is a well-documented fact that the thermal behaviour of people is contingent on the context (see for example, Williamson and Riordan 1997; Nicol 2001). This means that it can never be assumed that people in a low rating house will behave the same if placed in a high rating house. Because the differences in behaviour will most likely effect energy consumption, there is no logical way that the *potential* to reduce energy consumption makes sense and can be tested.

Given the apparent importance placed on HERS in national policies it is perhaps surprising to find so little written about them, and almost no work that investigates the claims that HERS save energy and costs and reduce greenhouse gas emissions. In one of the few research studies that have investigated the US HERS, Stein (1997) came to the conclusion that 'none of the HERS we examined showed any clear relationship between overall rating score and actual energy use or cost' (Stein 1997: 61).

Of the several HERS Stein examined, some overestimated the gas and electricity use by as much as 100 per cent. He noted that in many instances the take-back effect seemed to be operating in that, rather than reducing energy consumption, the occupants instead chose to increase their level of thermal comfort.

A study in Australia of NatHERS found no significant correlation between actual household heating and cooling energy use (or greenhouse gas emission) and ratings, and reached a similar finding in that 'the commonly held purpose of NatHERS, that higher Star Ratings will mean reduced household energy consumption and greenhouse gas emissions, could not be corroborated' (Williamson, O'Shea and Menadue 2001).

This finding is not really surprising because the NatHERS rating is related to the sum of the heating and cooling energy *loads* (that is, the efficiencies and fuel types for the heating and cooling appliances are not included in the assessment) therefore the scheme *does not* and *cannot* address directly the issues of energy use, greenhouse gas emissions or cost-effectiveness. In the US, the Home Energy Rating Systems also suffer from this problem. Since the 1992 Energy Policy Act HERS have been required to 'take into account local climate conditions and construction practices, solar energy collected on-site, and the benefits of peak load shifting construction practices, and not discriminate among fuel types' (US Energy Policy Act 1992). This requirement to be fuel neutral has meant that the development of a meaningful HERS has been constrained by the competing interests of the electric and gas industries. Fairey, Tait, *et al.* (2000) suggest that 'the effort to find a solution that is equitable and fuel neutral has proven to be a quest not unlike that for the Holy Grail'. A normalized modified loads method was adopted in 1999 (NASEO 2000) but since this method (like the Australian NatHERS) is based on energy loads and not an estimate of actual site energy it is unlikely to achieve energy savings, let alone a reduction in GHG emissions. Being fuel neutral, the HERS methodology has at its foundation an incomplete problem definition and is therefore incapable of differentiating between different fuels. Total house design solutions that incorporate low energy natural means of conditioning or renewable sources of energy are most likely discriminated against.

Only the UK SAP Carbon Index (CI) makes any attempt to relate the HERS rating directly to GHG emissions. The CI is based on the CO_2 emissions associated with space and water heating, but adjusted for floor area so that it is essentially independent of dwelling size for a given built form. The CI therefore gives no indication of the absolute CO_2 emission and a large dwelling and a small dwelling may have the same CI but cause very different CO_2 output.

If these concerns were not enough, a further failure to properly define the objective at hand could mean that well-meaning architects following HERS design advice (or being required to comply with a HERS) may in fact be contributing to excessive GHG emissions. Defining the problem more correctly as 'reducing the life cycle non-renewable energy consumption and/or life cycle GHG emissions', the embodied energy of the building materials and energy used to construct the building must be considered. Several studies taking this approach show that HERS often encourage the wrong solution. An analysis by Henriksen (2001) of a house in Newcastle, Australia, showed by LCA that of twenty strategies advocated in design guides to increase the NatHERS rating (and thereby, it is suggested, reduce energy consumption and GHG emissions), only insulating the roof and walls was likely to be justifiable in combined environmental and economic terms. Another study looking at the implications of different types of house construction for Sydney and Melbourne, Australia, showed that lightweight construction incorporating timber frames and timber cladding had the potential over a fifty year life of the building to reduce CO_2 emissions by around 20 per cent compared to the heavyweight brick construction rated most highly by NatHERS. A similar finding came out of a project conducted at the University of East London. Here the life cycle CO_2 emissions were estimated using computer simulation for heavyweight and lightweight houses for five locations in the UK. Because the embodied CO_2 of the lightweight timber framed construction was substantially lower than the alternative traditional brick construction, while at the same time the annual heating energy CO_2 showed little difference, overall the life cycle results favoured the lightweight construction (Smithdale and Thompson 2000).

The appropriate objectives

The public faith invested in HERS is admirable, but unless they are effectively addressing clearly stated objectives they are likely to be worse than useless in promoting good dwelling design. As we have seen in Chapter 4, addressing only parts of problems leads generally to ignorance and the misallocation of resources. The concentration on energy requirements in the name of addressing climate change is a legacy of the discourse from the 1970s and 1980s. Although connected with the contemporary issue of GHG emissions, it relates essentially to a different objective – conservation of energy required to operate buildings. Dealing with energy use is necessary but is not sufficient if we are to tackle reducing possible climate change. Concentrating on misconstrued objectives, and associated means, obscures dealing in a meaningful and holistic way with the issue of sustainable building design.

For Vitruvius there was a relatively simple relationship between building design and climate and his concern was with creating a pleasant internal environment. Today a pleasant environment is just as important, but we also know that achieving this objective can have implications far beyond the building itself. We understand in some detail many of the climatic variables that contribute to a pleasant environment, and we are beginning to appreciate how pursuing the objective of a pleasant environment by certain means can possibly affect the climate. Sustainable designing means taking responsibility to anticipate the wide consequences of a building proposal. Believing that all publicly endorsed codes of practice are sufficient to give the answers, to put things in order, is mistaken. No attempt to accommodate the real complexities of the world in neat regulations will lead to a sustainable architecture, and the complexity of each project needs to be considered in its context. To aid in decision-making we can employ, for example, life cycle assessment (LCA) techniques to help us anticipate many affects. If GHG emission was the (or a) dominant environmental issue, then in the LCA we would tackle that issue, and not an inadequate substitute. We would estimate the amount and type of energy to be used to produce the building materials and the fossil fuel derived energy that would be employed to run the building (for services such as lighting, heating and cooling, fans, transport, etc.), then we could determine the likely CO_2 emissions. We would most likely investigate incorporating renewable, non-polluting energy sources into the design solution. A thorough assessment would test the sensitivity of all assumptions to describe a range of outcomes. We would also identify and attempt to quantify all other environmental impacts that could be attributed to any aspect of the construction and use of the proposed building, and consider these in conjunction with social aspects, such as balancing needs against appropriate thermal comfort conditions, and economic questions such as the initial and operating costs. Avoiding the consequences of design decisions by merely conforming to public policy is a feature of a non-sustainable architecture. A sustainable architecture on the other hand will be a cohesive and creative adaptation to the context based on a private morality to perform a *beautiful* act.

Notes

1 For example, *Design with Climate* (Olgyay and Olgyay 1963), *Buildings, Climate and Energy* (Markus and Morris 1980), *Man, Climate and Architecture* (Givoni 1976).
2 A joint implementation approach was accepted in June 1998 by the European Union countries, known as the EU Bubble. The EU Bubble is designed to recognize differential targets within the EU. The EU's internal goals range from a 27 per cent increase for Portugal to 28 per cent cuts for Luxembourg, and 21 per cent cuts for Germany and Denmark. France and Finland are not required to have any cuts from the base year of 1990.
3 As of March 2002.
4 An Editorial in *The Guardian* (London), 24 July 2001 p. 19 stated: 'But most credit must go to the innumerable independent pressure groups, scientists and individual campaigners who, in the years that followed the 1992 Rio earth summit, made global warming an issue that governments could simply no longer ignore.'
5 In 1995 approximately 72 per cent of electricity in France was generated from nuclear power.
6 Many countries have inconsistent policies. Australia has no nuclear power, exports uranium 'because if we don't, someone else will', and restricts the number of mines and the initial destinations for the material.

7   Cohesion

From the preceding discussions it is clear that in seeking sustainable architecture there is no unequivocal course of action that will suit all ethical stances, all objectives and all situations. There is no class or style of design which is unequivocally sustainable architecture, and no fixed set of rules which will guarantee success if followed. Rather, there are difficult interrelated decisions to be made that are contingent on particular circumstances. There are many stakeholders, many objectives, and many sources of advice. There is much uncertainty. Nevertheless, we now need to focus on how we can recognize a sustainable building design in our own, or others' work, which carries with it the implied further question of how an architect can act morally in her or his professional sphere in relation to sustainability.

How, then, should we look at a building, at architecture as a cultural product that needs to be judged as an integrated entity while recognizing that it is simultaneously 'coming from' multiple origins and objectives? The key is social practices rather than technological fixes, and we should not divorce environmental sustainability from economic and sociocultural sustainability – the triple bottom line. It helps if we keep this view of a building as a response to many disparate requirements and origins high in our consciousness, in contrast to the prevalent architectural notion of the dominant unitary concept as the generating source of good building. Buildings cannot be pure expressions of sustainability because that is never the sole objective, the sole reason for their existence. Indeed a pure expression of sustainability may often be not to build at all. A building is always full of compromises, the result of juggling and trying to make compatible the diverse objectives of its creation. Fredric Jameson (1994: 168)[1] refers to a 'lumber room' in which complete and incomplete ideas, technical solutions, references to the past, and half-formed concepts – 'a kind of anthology of disconnected parts and pieces' – find themselves. The designer's task is to create a work in which the contents of the lumber room appear to be an integrated whole, a kind of post-rationalization in which an aesthetic object is made and legitimated. In the most successful buildings the work appears both aesthetically and functionally convincing, even inevitable, as a consequence of all its disparate origins. While unifying the differences in form, however, such works may not totally obscure the fractures, leaving apparent the inherent contradictions in a coexistence of different goals.

Responsive cohesion

If we accept this notion of the work of architecture as anthology rather than pure expression of concept, we open possibilities of looking closely at the way the parts of the anthology come together and interact with each other. Of course we are interested in building form and shading to get benefit from passive solar heating, in the possibilities of rooftop solar cells, in the embodied energy of the materials we are using. But we are interested in other ideas and issues as well. Our skill lies in acknowledging all of these, and creating a work in which the multitude of ideas and issues – the contents of the lumber room – respond to each other in convincing ways. And not only to each other, because our work also needs to respond to its wider context.

Warwick Fox uses the term 'responsive cohesion' to describe a state in which the various elements of a 'thing' (design work, community, creature) or process (design, construction, etc.) exhibit a reciprocal interaction between elements that constitute it, and the context in which it is located. The adjective responsive refers to the way in which the elements of the thing respond to the challenges set by other elements: responses to the claims of different stakeholders in a design process, or to the impacts of different building elements in a design work. The noun cohesion refers to the way that the result holds together: mutual accommodation in a design process, or a sense of unity in a design work. Responsive cohesion contrasts with domination by one factor, pattern or force, and equally with the absence of any cohesion, where work or process appear anarchic and uncontrolled (Fox 2000: 219). In the context of sustainable architecture, the various elements of the design will be responding to the objectives of the programme and the means for the production of a building.[2] It also suggests that the architect will be more of a pluralist than a formal purist.

Place, people and stuff

Fox argues that upholding the principle of responsive cohesion in sustainable architecture entails responding to ecological, social and built contexts, in that order of priority (Fox 2000: 225). Similarly, architect Paul Pholeros characterizes architecture as concerned with place, people and stuff, in that order, which shows agreement about priorities between architect and philosopher. These labels should be interpreted broadly, so that place or ecological concerns embrace all scales of place, from local building site to global ecological system. They follow from the themes of earlier chapters in this book. 'Social or people' concerns includes human health and well-being in a broad sense, too, including economic well-being. 'Stuff' is the materials, construction techniques, and services that make a building. The emphasis on order is important. Returning to our discussion of ethical positions in Chapter 3, the orthodox anthropocentric position in both architecture and philosophy would have put the social context ahead of the ecological context.[3] Putting ecological first illustrates the degree to which environmental concerns have moved to the forefront. Architecture is

7.1 Seeking cohesion: between the inner and outer skins of the Forest EcoCentre, Scotsdale, Tasmania, 2002 (architects Robert Morris-Nunn and Associates). The brief reflected 'the close links of the community and its industry to the environment and a desire for a sustainable future' (Forest EcoCentre visitor information brochure) (photographer Antony Radford).

most obviously manifested in the third concern, the stuff or built context, including the aesthetical tectonics of space and form as well as building and landscape materials. Indeed, conventionally architecture would put concern about stuff first, and placing this last in the order corresponds to a view of the issue as what can architecture mean for sustainability rather than vice versa; in other words how can the stuff of architecture be mobilized to advance our sustainability objectives for the environment and society.

While Fox puts the construction of this reasoned argument in the forefront, Susannah Hagan, in *Taking Shape: A New Contract Between Architecture and Nature* emphasizes the qualities of design proposals and sets out three criteria for generating sustainable architecture. They are symbiosis, differentiation and visibility (Hagan 2001: 98). Symbiosis refers to the relationship between building and nature, the ways in which these systems will work together for mutual benefit. Nature benefits the building through solar energy, site, materials and a host of other provisions. If we exclude the human race, it is harder to see how building might benefit nature beyond providing habitat for a small number of species of flora and fauna. Differentiation refers to the recognition of, and response to, the particularities of geographic and cultural place. Symbiosis and differentiation here correspond quite closely to the natural image and the cultural image that we describe in Chapter 2. Visibility refers to the symbolic and aesthetic emblems that we also briefly discussed in Chapter 2, the assertion that a building should visibly and overtly reflect its commitment to sustainability. All of these criteria are compatible with responsive cohesion.

These three contexts of ecology, society and building, then, constitute the frame within which design takes place. They do, of course, map closely on to the three popular images of sustainability – nature, culture, and technology – that we described in Chapter 2. The responsibility of the designer is to create a design that exhibits responsive cohesion in not just one but all of these contexts. We can look at this as the construction of a reasoned argument that weaves together the ethical, human, scientific, aesthetic and other aspects of these three contexts. If an architect can do this, taking into account all of the stakeholders, she or he is performing a *beautiful* act, as outlined at the end of Chapter 2.

Reflective practice and reasoned argument

This weaving takes place within reflective practice. The process of designing sustainable architecture is one of research, experience, making use of advice and information, negotiation and consensus. This, indeed, is the process of making any architecture: a to and fro between ethical theory, the environmental, social and building contexts, and personal and stakeholder evaluations.[4] How do we know that we are doing it successfully, or at least thoroughly? We are more likely to be doing both if we can make a reasoned and defensible argument for the responsive cohesion of whatever designs are made, an argument constructed by individuals or by design teams. Usually it will be a combination of individual and collective action. Ethically, this reasoned argument is necessary for self- and group-confidence that appropriate decisions have been made or are being made. Legally, the process may be reflected in requirements for the documentation of reasoned arguments in environmental impact statements (EIS). This provides the external assurance that such an argument has been constructed and the basis for independent auditing. But we have to accept that we are likely to be dealing with different constructions of situations involving incommensurable objectives and heavily dependent on values and ethics; performing *beautiful* acts is not easy.

It follows from this assertion of the importance of reasoned argument that performance specifications for new development along the lines of environmental impact statements should be required for major building developments, combining environmental, social and cultural sustainability. The EIS audit is a way that allows best practice to develop, rather than defining best practice. It focuses on the process, rather than on a product specification.

Credibility, transferability, dependability and confirmability

Reasoned argument, though, does not sound like an end point. If this book appears to suggest that everything is acceptable as long as a reasoned argument can be produced, then any transformative effect will be manifest in documentation and bureaucratic procedures rather than in buildings. We need a way of distinguishing sound from spurious reasoned argument. In the positivist world of the sciences and quantifiable measurements there are established criteria of 'internal validity, external validity, reliability and objectivity' (Guba and Lincoln 1989: 234). Where the argument extends to non-quantitative, subjective and cultural issues the ground is less clear.

Since the issue is essentially one of credibility and trust, the labels for the set of trustworthiness criteria developed by Guba and Lincoln in relation to non-positivist (including social constructivist) research methodologies provide guidance. They are credibility, transferability, dependability and confirmability (Guba and Lincoln 1989: 236–43). As those authors use them, they are more applicable to design advice (as the result of design research – see below) than the results of design generation, but the labels can be appropriated for our purposes. Credibility will derive from extensive engagement, negative case analysis (in our case investigating alternative design options and finding inferior results), and appropriate authority. Transferability is a cue for checking that those appeals to appropriate authority are indeed relevant: in Guba and Lincoln's words, that 'salient conditions overlap and match' (Guba and Lincoln 1989: 241). Dependability requires that the argument is complete, allowing the reader (or reflective designer) to follow and understand it without unexplained leaps from argument to conclusion. Confirmability 'requires one to show the way in which interpretations have been arrived at' (Koch 1994: 978), and in our context requires the presentation of raw versions of sources for the argument as well as of the design. All this sounds like an enormous amount of work, but expectations are related to the scale of the project and its potential impact. A public Environmental Impact Statement (EIS) for a major development will have a character very different from an architect's self-reflective argument about a small facet of a private house, even if the need for reasoned argument and the criteria of trustworthiness remain essentially the same.

It is important to note this sameness of process at very different degrees of complexity. Perhaps a way of looking at this is by thinking of the difference between expertise and wisdom. We can imagine expertise as quantifiable (more expertise, higher expertise) and privatized as intellectual property, so that the ability to produce sustainable architecture becomes a commodity which can be offered only by large transnational professional practices.[5] The expertise to handle a complex project effectively may indeed reside in a large multidisciplinary practice, although it may also be available through the temporary association of smaller groups. Wisdom is the ability to make good use of knowledge, a quality of individuals manifested in actions. To be wise does not require us to join big business. Wisdom without expertise is always better than expertise without wisdom – we can always seek out the necessary expertise, but the unwise rarely realize what is missing.

Turning to the question of recognizing sustainable architecture, Fox addresses this simply and directly by referring back to the design process: in what ways does the building exhibit responsive cohesion, remembering the priorities of ecological, social, and built contexts? Susannah Hagan similarly refers back to design generation, with the three criteria of symbiosis, difference and visibility as the means for identifying and assessing claims of architectural products to environmental sustainability (Hagan 2001: 98). And Guba and Lincoln's trustworthiness criteria of credibility, transferability, dependability and confirmability help in judging the validity of claims for sustainability in architecture and other products.

We argue, then, for the central role of reasoned argument in both making and recognizing sustainable architecture. The architect or design team works reflectively, questioning and justifying decisions. There is no conceptual difference between the small work and the big project. An architect working alone on a small project carries out a kind of mental EIS, satisfying herself or himself that the decisions are responsive, cohesive and defendable. A project team shares and develops this EIS to their mutual understanding and satisfaction. A major project requires this EIS to be presented in a formal way to an external audience for exposure and comment. In some circumstances reasoned argument may lead to a decision not to build at all, in others to build smaller, or to refurbish existing buildings rather than replace them. Higher architect fees and lower building budgets would reflect a truly careful and valued reasoning process.

Public policy and the status quo

Policies embody the values, and reflect the knowledge, of the time when they were written. They can be difficult to modify. The narrow range of images presented by current sources of design advice perpetuate a restrictive understanding of the nature of environmental issues associated with design and limit ideas about appropriate ways of addressing them. Much policy-making on environmental issues originates with representatives of government organizations, academic institutions and professional organizations. The practices of these organizations commonly reflect the technocratic belief that environmental change is not incompatible with the status quo, as in the technical image of architectural sustainability described in Chapter 2. Existing resource allocation, power supplies, transport systems, subdivision practices, lending policies of banks, building regulations, design methods, construction practices, lifestyles and modes of consumption are, in large part, accepted as inevitable. One of the difficulties with changing the status quo is that proposals for change usually address only an aspect of the whole, so that work continues within the same overall frame and expectations. Moreover, because change is piecemeal it has to be compatible with the overall frame and its principles, goals and strategies (Beach 1990: 54). Policy approaches are based on what has been done before or has previously been identified as appropriate. The net result is that things tend to continue much as they are, with change only at the margin even where there is commitment and motivation. Those changes that are considered to be possible and appropriate are consequently highly restricted, restricting the options available in making decisions. So in practice, design is better able to respond quickly to the here and now, and to envisage the future, than is policy development. Unlike policy strategies, architects' images can encompass the many contextual issues that affect a particular situation, and the interactions between these issues. Design is a creative activity. It involves the capacity to visualize new and different ways of doing things. We should not wait for policies to change. But policies are important in supporting and guiding design and development.

The way questions regarding environmental aspects of building are framed determines the issues that are considered important and therefore to be addressed during design. It also influences whether participants of the design process are considered to have an active role in the process, and the processes and outcomes that are deemed to be acceptable. Designers of design advice that seeks to support the consideration of environmental aspects of design should acknowledge the contextual nature of design, make aims and assumptions clear, and ensure that strategies and aims are matched. They should not be determining solutions – that is the domain of design – but should support the development of those solutions.

The future

What is considered to be appropriate in a building is itself a cultural construction and will reflect contemporary life, including predominant ethics and perceptions of the importance of sustainability. At times and places in the past the nature of building has been framed as using only locally available materials and skills, and sometimes using only regenerating materials. The nature of building has also been framed within assumptions of little energy use or services systems. Architecture is practised at doing the best that can be done with what is available and possible and buildings do not need to be environmentally irresponsible in order to be serious architecture.

Society's expectations of new buildings are changing, particularly in concert with a cultural shift in its view of nature. What was once acceptable and unremarked is now contentious. Change does not necessarily involve a sudden revolution; compare western society's changing attitudes to such diverse issues as gender equality, smoking, and the wearing of wild animal fur as a fashion item. It has been argued that changing attitudes to nature and unease about whether animals should be recognized as members of the moral class are apparent in lower per capita consumption of meat and increased concern for animal welfare as much as by numbers of avowed vegetarians. If people come to feel that 'it's not really very nice to eat animals' they are inclined to be less excessive in this 'not nice' behaviour. There is enough peer pressure within the culture of architecture now for architects to be uncomfortable with, if not ashamed of, being associated with the more obvious examples of energy profligacy or material waste.

But can architects really be far out of step with the attitudes and values of their clients and society in general? So far those architects who have overtly set out to design a more sustainable architecture have done so with the support of their clients. In some cases they may have won that support through their own reasoned argument, while in others the client may have taken the lead. But few clients are willing to pay significantly increased costs relative to other design options for (on a world scale) marginal environmental benefits. Further, industry does not believe that they will do so, and therefore often does not produce the kind of initially more expensive but more 'environmentally friendly' systems that might make a difference. The most effective spur for a more sustainable architecture by far would be if environmental impacts were *really* reflected in real costing, including environmental costing, of materials and energy. This will only happen in a market economy if the costs and benefits to the world are reflected in the costs and benefits to individuals, bringing the personal field of significance into line with the global field. To achieve this, the bottom-up transformation without coercion through cultural change will almost certainly need to operate in parallel with a top-down process of policy change driven by international obligations, as has been started – albeit contentiously and in too small a way – in the *Kyoto Protocol*.

We do not subscribe to a view that the future is one of returning to local, natural materials and traditional building forms. Rather, we expect technological advances in the harnessing of solar and wind energy, the integration of digital with physical environments, the recycling and efficient use and production of materials, and the control of services that will reframe the cultural understanding of a building's role and form. We should be able to – and can – do better than simply return to a past mode of architecture. The architect Nicholas Grimshaw said:

> Technology and the growth of computers allows you a much freer palette as an architect. Also, the study of nature and the way plants grow is more and more available. Bring these things together and there is quite a strong

human response. Combine with a better understanding of materials, then we are in for a much richer phase of architecture.[6]

Design skills will be honed and expertise developed to respond to contemporary situations. Some of the buildings that have been hailed as environmentally sustainable at the turn of the century will come to be regarded as naive, others as heralding the future. We need bold (but reasoned and justified) design experiments to continue. The work of Fathy, Foster, Grimshaw, Pearce, Yeang and others is important because it provides a series of reflective experiments in practice that continue from project to project. With varying degrees of commitment to evaluation and learning from experience, *every* designing architect is engaged in such a series of reflective experiments in practice. That is a way to learn and provide justification for further projects. We need to be suspicious of doomsayers, greenwash and culturewash in architecture as in other fields.

The consideration of environmental issues is a way to affirm what we value and to give meaning to our lives. Architectural design, along with other creative processes, is a vehicle that allows us to project into the future and to imagine what should be and how things could work. Architects can and do think about and deal with complex issues ranging over the global and the local, the individual and the public, the scientific and the artistic. Sustainability in architecture emphasizes the long term, the role of architecture (in concert with landscape architecture, urban design, planning, engineering, politics and a myriad of other human endeavours) in enabling the sustainability of our environment and society – a really significant creative challenge. And, returning to the opening paragraph of this book, understanding sustainable architecture is simply understanding architecture as it is framed in many (but not all) professional and national cultures at the start of the twenty-first century – and that involves, as always, understanding that there is no one version of this framing that everyone will accept.

We called this book *Understanding Sustainable Architecture*. We have stressed the cultural dependency and relativity of the term sustainability. There *is* no easy coherent 'it', no accepted and codified body of knowledge, to understand. We have argued that it is important to seek to understand the phenomena and concepts of architectural sustainability with all their contradictions. But that does not mean that we are neutral, that for us anything goes. Rather, we believe that given this plurality of understandings and diversity of means, a mental checklist for use in recognizing or designing buildings will concentrate on processes followed rather than design results (although in the case of recognition the process may need to be inferred from the result). Four steps are:

1   *Who or what are the stakeholders ('affected members of the moral class') in this situation?* Some stakeholders are obvious (clients, users, designers) while others are less obvious. In terms of environmental impacts, it may be better to think in terms of present and future ecosystems, social systems and landscapes than in terms of individuals. It is always important to think

about the bigger system of which the building or proposed building forms a part, and the role of the project in that bigger system.

2 *Given these stakeholders, what are meaningful design objectives for sustainable architecture?* Objectives may differ for different stakeholders. As decision-makers, we inevitably place priorities on objectives which reflect our values, but we should note the general hierarchy of ecological, social and built contexts.

3 *Given these and other design objectives, how was (or might be) responsive cohesion sought in the contexts of environment, society and building?* Responsive cohesion is not the same as compromise. It is the essence of designing, of trying to make a coherent whole out of many parts. The more extensive checklist in the Appendix connects stakeholders, issues and objectives with possible means for their achievement, but it does not assist with finding responsive cohesion in the unique contexts of any one design project.

4 *Can a reasoned argument be made for this responsive cohesion that passes the tests of credibility, transferability, dependability and confirmability?* This is an important final step, too often bypassed. There may be no guarantees, but there should at least be evidence.

If we take out the adjective 'sustainable' in our checklist, we find a list that applies to all architecture. If we go further, and take out the reference to architecture as well, we have a list that applies to all decisions: stakeholders, objectives, responsive cohesion, and defendable reasoned argument. So after all there is nothing unique about how we should approach the making and identification of sustainable architecture; this is the way good design should be. This is what we would expect if, returning to the very beginning of this book, it is a reconceptualization of architecture in response to a myriad of contemporary concerns about the effects of human activity. But this does not make it any easier. There are better and worse decisions that can be made, convincing and unconvincing arguments to support them, and fine and poor buildings to build (or not build). Performing *beautiful* acts, that is, making a truly (more) sustainable architecture, is indeed difficult, but we architects like to believe that we are good at designing our way out of difficult situations.

Notes

1 This appears in a discussion on the work of architects Rem Koolhaus and Peter Eisenman. Jameson notes Pierre Macherey's (1966) book *Towards a Theory of Literary Production* as providing a model for reading work that stems from multiple origins.

2 Here we assume a strong relationship between building form and environmental conditions, a kind of function. Alberto Pérez-Gómez refers back to the time 'prior to the nineteenth century' (and the rise of positivism and functionalism in architecture) when 'Not only did form not follow function, but form could fulfil its role as a primary means of reconciliation, one that referred ultimately to the essential ambiguity of the human condition' (Pérez-Gómez 1983: 7).

3 Paul Pholeros says he 'used to put the people first', but now considers the environmental issues of place to be paramount (personal communication).

4 The ethicist/political philosopher John Rawls (author of A *Theory of Justice*, 1972) refers to the process of going backwards and forwards between an ethical theory and personal evaluations in order to get some kind of acceptable balance as the process of 'reflective equilibrium', a similar concept to Fox's 'responsive cohesion'.

5 The technical image of sustainability (see Chapter 2) with its emphasis on scientific method and technological means of addressing objectives, particularly promotes this impression. Indeed, David Harvey notes that

> It is not impossible to imagine a world in which big industry (certain segments), big governments (including the World Bank), and establishment, high-tech big science can get to dominate the world even more than they currently do in the name of 'sustainability', ecological modernization, and appropriate global management of the supposedly fragile health of planet Earth.
>
> (Harvey 1998: 343)

6 In answer to a question at the RAIA National Conference, Cairns, Australia, October 1998.

Appendix
A partial checklist for sustainable architecture

Since architectural sustainability is a cultural construction, no checklist can be either objective or complete. This one is not an exception. It is included as a basis for discussion and adaptation in seeking cohesion, as discussed in Chapter 7. The column headings are drawn from the discussion of objectives, stakeholders and decision-making in Chapter 4. The five categories are drawn from the discussion of a systems view in Chapter 5. Appropriate product means should be assessed in terms of *all* the issues and stakeholders, and in terms of the *full* life cycle of the project (including production and disposal), and not just its in-use operation.

Discourse issue	Stakeholders	Objectives	Principal active stakeholders	Architects' possible process means	Aspects of possible product means	Notes
1 Environmental impact						
Climate change	Many existing ecosystems, present and future generations of people.	• Reduce life cycle greenhouse gas emissions • Create carbon sinks • Mitigate effects of possible climate change	Designers, clients, occupiers, government, builders, product manufacturers.	• Life cycle greenhouse gas analysis. • Work with client and occupiers on future operation of the building. • Work with client in considering the wider system of which the building is a part. • Work with builders and product manufacturers on production sources and processes.	*Consider:* • Reducing the need for heating and cooling through building form, materials, and control systems • Using forms of energy in the operation of the building that do not produce greenhouse gases • Using highly energy efficient appliances, water heating and space heating and cooling systems • Using materials and equipment where the use of fuels producing greenhouse gases in their extraction, manufacture and transport is low • Allowing for uncertain future climate • Planting trees.	• Credible local data for a life cycle greenhouse gas analysis is hard to find. • There are many published strategies for reducing the need for energy-using heating and cooling systems: shading, orientation, insulation, Trombe walls, ventilation chimneys, geo-thermal systems, double skin enclosures, etc. Remember local context, the 'credibility, transferability, dependability and confirmability' criteria, and the need for a life cycle (and not just operating) impact perspective. • Future climate change may effect rain, wind, temperatures etc.

Discourse issue	Stakeholders	Objectives	Principal active stakeholders	Architects' possible process means	Aspects of possible product means	Notes
Pollution	Many existing ecosystems, including present and future generations of people.	• Reduce acid rain • Reduce air pollution • Reduce water pollution • Reduce land pollution	Designers, clients, occupiers, government, builders, product manufacturers.	• Life cycle pollution impact analysis. • Work with client and occupiers on future operation of the building. • Work with client in considering the wider system of which the building is a part. • Work with builders and product manufacturers on production sources and processes.	*Consider reducing pollution during construction by:* • Reducing waste materials • Using components that have caused little pollution in extraction, manufacture and transport. *Consider reducing pollution during building operation by:* • Using non-polluting energy sources • Avoiding potential polluted surface water run-off • Recycling water. *Consider reducing pollution at end of building or component life by:* • Using long-life materials • Using biodegradable materials • Using recyclable materials.	• Credible local data for a pollution impact analysis is hard to find. • Reusing buildings (see longevity in section 5 of this Appendix) and building components is a significant means of reducing land fill. • The generation of nuclear energy creates no greenhouse gases, but does create potentially serious sources of pollution.
Resource depletion	Present and future generations of people.	Use resources wisely	Designers, clients, occupiers, government, builders, product manufacturers.	Determine renewability and rarity of resources.	*Consider:* • Using renewable resources (e.g. plantation timber, managed regrowth timber, solar energy) • Using plentiful resources (e.g. many building stones, clays, silicon, iron ore) • Very careful, appropriate use of rare and non-renewable resources • Building small.	• Adding intellectual value by good design while limiting resource use by building small may be an effective strategy for this and other environmental objectives.

					Consider:	
Biodiversity	Many existing ecosystems, including present and future generations of people.	Avoid actions that lead to reduction of biodiversity	Designers, clients, government, product manufacturers.	Determine what ecosystems are effected by the project, and how.	• Avoiding building in places that are particularly significant for biodiversity • Using timber with an authoritative certificate of origin • Shifting use of rainforest timbers to low-volume, high value applications • Creating landscapes rich in biodiversity.	• The reduction of rainforest is often cited as the most urgent issue in maintaining biodiversity. • Consider water- as well as land-based ecosystems.
Indigenous flora and fauna	Local non-human ecosystems	• Minimize disturbance to local flora and fauna • Maintain viability of local ecosystems	Designers, owners, government.	Analyse existing local ecosystems.	*Consider:* • Minimal building footprint • Minimal disturbance to surrounding vegetation • Leaving wildlife movement corridors • Designing to avoid bird strikes on windows, wind turbines, etc.	There are places where the appropriate *overall* decision is not to build at all.

2 Social and cultural relevance

					Consider:	
Society and culture	People	• Reflect and express culture • Relate built form to social and economic activity • Maintain significant building heritage values • Create future heritage value	Design professionals, owners, government.	• Consult with local community about buildings and urban patterns that are socially and culturally relevant to it. • Work with government on the development of appropriate development and heritage guidelines. • Invite peer and public review.	• Using locally-sourced materials • Designing to enable the use of locally-sourced skills for construction and future maintenance • Adapting existing buildings • Maintaining existing mix of spaces for living, trade and social activities • Maintaining existing scale and typologies of buildings • Emphasizing public space • Respecting existing built context • Using pre-used 'blighted' sites rather than green field sites.	• Achieving a balance between continuity and vitality is central to this issue. • The culture or society for which relevance is sought may not be a geographically-defined entity or group. • There is much published advice about strategies for community consultation.

Discourse issue	Stakeholders	Objectives	Principal active stakeholders	Architects' possible process means	Aspects of possible product means	Notes
3 Occupants						
Health	Occupants and neighbouring people	Healthy people	Designers, clients, government.	Assess potential health impacts of design decisions.	*Consider:* • Designing for high fresh air change rate (above minimum requirements) • Using materials with authoritative guarantees of non-toxicity • Designing for easy cleaning and maintenance.	Health problems can arise through lack of anticipated maintenance – consider the likelihood and effects of breakdown in expected maintenance regimes.
Comfort	Occupants	• Thermal comfort • Visual comfort • Aural comfort	Designers, clients, government.	Determine context-related preferences for 'comfort'.	*Consider:* • Designing so that the building itself offers internal conditions that are within or approach culturally acceptable limits • Using energy-using systems only when appropriate in relation to other sustainability issues.	• Perceptions of, and preferences for, comfort levels vary quite widely. • Preferences in the trade-off between comfort and other qualities, such as indoor-outdoor links, also vary widely. • Acceptable variations in conditions partly depend on whether occupants are able to change activity and/or location in response to feelings of discomfort.

4 Economic performance

Cost effectiveness	Clients, (other) people	• Net benefit • Return on investment	Designers, financiers, clients, builders, government.	• Determine life cycle costs • Work with client in considering wider objectives and whether building is the best way to meet those objectives • Recognize expertise of builder in cost-effective design • Consider how uncertainty in economic conditions may effect building use and life • Cost planning and control.	*Consider:* • Designing for low imported energy use • Design for low maintenance.	Also note the process and product means for longevity (see section 5 of this Appendix).

5 The building

Longevity	Clients, (other) people	• Durability • Adaptability • Serviceability • Maintainability	Designers, clients, government	• Consult possible future users • Seek flexibility in interpretation of fit between use and building • Work with client on asset management plan.	*Consider:* • Adapting and using existing building stock rather than building new • Designing for adaptability and future change of use • Using long-life materials • Allowing provision for possible future services • Using measures to protect from place-dependant risks such as bush fires and corrosive seaside air • Designing for low maintenance and easy serviceability • Allowing for uncertainty in future climate.	The potential physical life of a building may be much longer than its economic, functional, social, legal (e.g. changing fire, earthquake or disability access codes) or technological life. Buildings 'die' because they are deemed to be obsolete in any of these aspects. Moreover, (as with humans) death typically occurs when only a part of the building fails.

Bibliography

Adams, R. M. (1997) 'Should ethics be more impersonal?', in J. Dancy (ed.) *Reading Parfit*, Oxford: Blackwell Publishers.

AGO (1999) *Australian commercial building sector greenhouse gas emissions 1990–2010*, Canberra: Australian Greenhouse Office.

Alexander, C. (1987) *A New Theory of Urban Design*, New York: Oxford University Press.

APHA (1939) *The basic principles of healthful housing*, Committee on hygiene and healthful housing, Washington: American Public Health Association.

Aristotle (1962) *Nicomachean Ethics*, trans by M. Ostwald, Indianapolis: Bobbs-Merrill Co.

Arnheim, R. (1993) 'Sketching and the psychology of design', *Design Issues* IX(2): 15–19.

Baier, K. (1969) 'What is value?', in K. Baier and N. Rescher (eds) *Values and the Future: The Impact of Technological Change on American Values*, New York: New York Free Press.

Baird, G. (2001) *The Architectural Expression of Environmental Control Systems*, London and New York: Spon Press.

Baron, J. (1988) *Thinking and Deciding*, New York: Cambridge University Press.

Bauman, Z. (1993) *PostModern Ethics*, Oxford: Blackwell Publishers.

Bauman, Z. (1995) *Life in Fragments: Essays in PostModern Morality*, Oxford: Blackwell Publishers.

Bauman, Z. (2001) *The Individualized Society*, Cambridge: Polity Press.

Beach, L. R. (1990) *Image Theory: Decision Making in Personal and Organizational Contexts*, Chichester: John Wiley and Sons.

Bengs, C. (1993) 'Sustainable development – end or action?', in T. Oksala (ed.) *Design: Ecology, Aesthetics, Ethics, Proceedings of DEcon '93 Special Focus Symposium of Intersymp '93*, Baden-Baden: The International Institute for Systems Research and Cybernetics.

Bennett, R. J. and Chorley, R. J. (1978) *Environmental Systems: Philosophy, Analysis and Control*, London: Methuen.

Bennetts, H. (2000) 'Environmental issues and house design in Australia: images from theory and practice', unpublished thesis, University of Adelaide.

Blachère, G. (1971) 'Human requirements', *Proceedings of the 5ᵗʰ Congress on Research into Practice*, Paris-Versailles: International Council for Building Research, Studies and Documentation.

Boulding, K. E. (1961) *The Image: Knowledge in Life and Society*, Michigan: The University of Michigan Press.

Boulding, K. E. (1978) *Ecodynamics: A New Theory of Societal Evolution*, Beverly Hills, California: Sage Publications.

Buchanan, R. (1992) 'Wicked problems in design thinking', *Design Issues* VIII(2): 5–21.

Bush, G. W. (2002) *President Announces Clear Skies and Global Climate Change Initiatives, 14 February 2002*, Online. Available HTTP: <http://www.whitehouse.gov/news/releases/2002/02/20020214-5.html> (March 2002).

CEBS (1949) 'Design for climate: some notes on the design of domestic buildings for the hot arid and hot humid climates of Australia', *Notes on the Science of Building*, No. 1, Sydney: Commonwealth Experimental Building Station.

Coldicutt, S. and Williamson, T. J. (1995) 'The limits of instrumentalism', *Proceedings of ANZAScA Conference*, University of Canberra, Canberra: Australian and New Zealand Architectural Science Association.

Cole, R. L. (1997) 'Prioritizing environmental criteria in building design and assessment', in P. S. Brandon, P. L. Lombardi and V. Bentivegna (eds) *Evaluation of the Built Environment for Sustainability*, London: E. & F. N. Spon.

Cole, R. J. and Larsson, N. (2000) GBC 2000 Assessment manual: Volume 1 – Overview, Online. Available HTTP: <http://buildingsgroup.NRCan.gc.ca/Projects_e/GBTool.html> (March 2002).

Commonwealth of Australia (1997) *Climate Change: Australia's Second National Report under the United Nations Framework Convention on Climate Change*, Online. Available HTTP: <http://unfccc.int/resource/docs/natc/ausnc2.pdf> (March 2002).

Cooper, D. E. (1992) 'The idea of environment' in D. E. Cooper and J. A. Palmer (eds) *The Environment in Question: Ethics and Global Issues*, London: Routledge.

Crawley, D. and Aho, I. (1999) 'Building environmental assessment methods: applications and development trends', *Building Research and Information*, 27(4/5): 300–8.

CSDCP (1996) *Central Sydney Development Control Plan Environmental management policy*, Online. Available HTTP: <www.cityofsydney.nsw.gov.au/pdf/catz_ditc_city_plan_csdcp_csdcp_part04_environmental_management_0101.pdf> (February 2002).

Curwell, S. and Spencer, L. (1999) *Environmental assessment of buildings: survey of W100*. Salford: University of Salford Research Centre for the Built and Human Environment.

Daly, H. E. (1993) 'Sustainable growth: an impossibility theorem' in H. E. Daly and K. N. Townsend (eds) *Valuing the Earth*, Cambridge, Massachusetts: MIT Press.

Daly, H. E. (1999) *Ecological economics and the Ecology of Economics*, Cheltenham: Edward Elgar.

Daniels, K. (1995) *The technology of ecological building*, Basel: Birkhäuser Verlag.

Day, C. (2000) 'Ethical building in the everyday environment. A multilayer approach to building and place design', in W. Fox (ed.) *Ethics in Building*, London: Routledge.

Des Jardins, J. R. (2001) *Environmental Ethics: An Introduction to Environmental Philosophy*, 3rd Edn, California: Wadsworth/Thomson Learning.

Downing, F. (1992a) 'Image banks: dialogues between the past and the future', *Environment and Behaviour* 24(4): 441–70.

Downing, F. (1992b) 'Conversations in imagery', *Design Studies* 13(3): 291–319.

Downing, F. (1994) 'Memory and the making of places', in K. A. Franck and L. H. Schneekloth (eds), *Ordering Space: Types in Architecture and Design*, New York: Van Nostrand Reinhold.

Dripps, R. D. (1999) *The First House: Myth, Paradigm and the Task of Architecture*, Cambridge, Massachusetts: MIT Press.

Dubos, R. (1976) *A God Within: A Positive View of Mankind's Future*, London: Abacus.

Durand, J-N-L. (1801) *Recueil et Paralléle des Edifices de Tout Genre, Anciens et Modernes*, Paris: École Polytechnique.

Durand, J-N-L. (1802) *Précis des Leçons d'Architecture*, Paris: École Polytechnique.

Elliot, R. (1991) 'Environmental ethics', in P. Singer (ed.) *A Companion to Ethics*, Oxford, UK: Blackwell Publishers.

Encyclopaedia Britannica (1998) Multimedia Edition, on CD.

EPA (2000) *Framework for Responsible Environmental Decision-Making (FRED): Using Life Cycle Assessment to Evaluate Preferability of Products*, Cincinnati, Ohio: US Environment Protect Agency, Online. Available HTTP: <http://www.epa.gov/oamhpod1/oppts_grp/0100023/fred.pdf> (December 2001).

Fairey, P., Tait, J., Goldstein, D., Tracey, D., Holtz, M. and Judkoff, R. (2000) *The HERS Rating Method and the Derivation of the Normalized Modified Loads Method*, Research Report No. FSEC-RR-54-00, Cocoa, FL: Florida Solar Energy Center, Online. Available HTTP: <http://www.fsec.ucf.edu/_bdac/pubs/hers_meth/rr54.html> (December 2001).

Fawcett, A. P. (1998) 'Twenty-twenty vision', *Journal of Southeast Asian Architecture*, 3(1): 57–72.

Fawcett, A. P. and Lim G. T. (1998) 'Embodied energy concepts: relevance to lightweight structures', paper presented at LSA98, Lightweight Structures in Architecture, Engineering and Construction International Congress, Sydney.

Feldman, F. (1998) 'Kantian ethics', in J. P. Sterba (ed.) *Ethics: The Big Questions*, Malden, Massachusetts: Blackwell.

Fisher, J. (1994) 'A global perspective', *Perspectives*, 1(6): 32–3.

Foliente, G. (1998) *Paper prepared for the International Council for Research and Innovation in Building and Construction (CIB)*, Online. Available HTTP: <http://www.cibworld.nl/pages/ib/9902/pages/notesgs.html#anchor141490> (January 2002).

Forrester, J. W. (1968) *Principles of Systems*, 2nd edn, Cambridge, Massachusetts: Wright-Allen Press.

Foster, J. (ed.) (1997) *Valuing Nature?: Ethics, Economics and the Environment*, London: Routledge.

Foster, N. (1999) Interview broadcast on BBC Radio 4, May.

Foucault, M. (1972) *The Archaeology of Knowledge*, London: Travistock.

Foucault, M. (1997) *Ethics: Subjectivity and Truth*, (ed.) P. Rabinow trans. R. Hurley, New York: New Press.

Fox, W. (1991) *Toward a Transpersonal Ecology*, Boston: Shambhala.

Fox, W. (2000) 'Towards an ethics (or at least a value theory)', in W. Fox (ed.) *Ethics and the Built Environment*, London: Routledge.

Fukuyama, F. (1992) *The End of History and the Last Man*, New York: Free Press.

Georgescu-Roegen, N. (1993) 'Selections from energy and economic myths' in H. E. Daly and K. N. Townsend (eds) *Valuing the Earth: Economy, Ecology, Ethics*, Cambridge, Massachusetts: MIT Press. Reprinted from *Southern Economic Journal* 41:3 (1975).

Giddens, A. (1999a) *BBC Reith Lecture 2*. Online. Available HTTP: <http://news6.thdo.bbc.co.uk/hi/english/static/events/reith_99/week2/week2.htm> (March 2002).

Giddens, A. (1999b) *BBC Reith Lecture 3 – Tradition*. Online. Available HTTP: <http://news6.thdo.bbc.co.uk/hi/english/static/events/reith_99/week3.htm> (March 2002).

Givoni, B. (1976) *Man, Climate and Architecture*, 2nd edn, London: Applied Science.

Glendinning, I. (1996) 'Ku-ring-gai councils energy efficiency housing policy' in *Proceedings of 2nd National Energy Efficient Building and Planning Seminar*, Wollongong: Paraclete Building Consultants.

Greece (1997) *Second National Communication to the UNFCCC*, Online. Available HTTP: <http://unfccc.int/resource/docs/natc/grenc2.pdf> (March 2002).

Greenhough, H. (1947) 'Relative and independent beauty' in H. A. Small (ed.) *Form and Function*, Berkeley and Los Angeles: University of California Press.

Greer, J. and Bruno, K. (1996) *Greenwash: The Reality Behind Corporate Environmentalism*, Penang: Third World Network and New York: Apex Press.

Gross, J. G. (1996) 'Developments in the application of the performance concept in building', in *Proceedings of the 3rd International Symposium on Applications of the Performance Concept in Building*, Tel-Aviv: CIB-ASTM-ISO-RILEM. Online. Available HTTP: <http://www.cibworld.nl/pages/ib/9701/pages/17.htm> (accessed January 2002).

Guba, E. G. and Lincoln, Y. S. (1989) *Fourth Generation Evaluation*, Newbury Park, California: Sage Publications.

Guy, S. and Farmer, G. (2000) 'Contested constructions: the competing logics of green buildings and ethics', in Warwick Fox (ed.) *Ethics and the Built Environment*, London and New York: Routledge.

Guy, S. and Farmer, G. (2001) 'Reinterpreting sustainable architecture: The place of technology', *Journal of Architectural Education*, 54(3): 140–8.

Habermas, J. (1990) *Moral Consciousness and Communicative Action*, trans C. Lenhardt and S. W. Nicholsen, Cambridge, Massachusetts: MIT Press.

Hagan, S. (2001) *Taking Shape: A New Contract Between Architecture and Nature*, London: Architectural Press.

Haider, S. G. and Khachaturian, N. (1972) 'A systems approach for the evaluation of the performance of buildings in the design process', in *National Bureau of Standards special publication 361: Proceedings of the joint RILEM-ASTM-CIB symposium*, Philadelphia: US Department of Commerce.

Haila, Y. and Levins, R. (1992) *Humanity and Nature: Ecology, Science and Society*. London: Pluto Press.

Hajer, M. A. (1995) *The Politics of Environmental Discourse*. Oxford: Oxford University Press.

Harries, K. (1997) *The Ethical Function of Architecture*, Cambridge, Massachusetts: MIT Press.

Harris, R. (1991) *A Space for Dreaming, A Different Reality*, Jarrow: Bede Gallery.

Hartland Thomas, M. (1948) 'The influence of technical research on design and methods of building', *RIBA Journal*, 55(5): 188–92.

Harvey, D. (1998) 'What's green and makes the environment go round? Socialism and environmental politics' in Frederic Jameson and Maso Miyoshi (eds) *The Cultures of Globalization*, Durham and London: Duke University Press.

Heating and Ventilation (Reconstruction) Committee (1945) *Heating and Ventilation of Dwellings* (Post-War Building Studies Report No. 19 of the Building Research Board of the Department of Scientific and Industrial Research), London: HMSO for the Ministry of Works.

Heidegger, M. (1971) 'Building, Dwelling, Thinking', in *Poetry, Language, Thought*, trans and introduction by A. Hofstadter, New York: Harper and Row Publishers.

Henriksen, J. (2001) 'Life cycle analysis for energy accounting in residential architecture', in W. Osterhaus and J. McIntosh (eds), *Proceedings of the 35th ANZAScA Conference*. School of Architecture, Victoria University of Wellington, NZ: Australia and New Zealand Architectural Science Association (Published on CD).

Herring, H. (1999) 'Does energy efficiency save energy? The debate and its consequences', *Applied Energy*, 63: 209–26.

Hillier, B. and Penn, A. (1994) 'Virtuous circles, building sciences and the science of buildings: using computers to integrate product and processes in the built environment', *Design Studies*, 15(3): 332–65.

Hodgson, P. (2001) Reported in *The Guardian* (London), 24 July, p1.

Holland, G. and Holland, I. (1995) 'Difficult decisions about ordinary things: being ecologically responsible about timber framing', *Australian Journal of Environmental Management* 2(3): 157–72.

Houghton, J. (1998) 'The christian challenge of caring for the earth', *JRI Briefing Paper No. 1*, Online. Available HTTP: <http://www.jri.org.uk/brief/christianchallenge.htm> (February 2002).

HRH The Prince of Wales (2000) *BBC Reith Lecture 6*, Online. Available HTTP: <http://news6.thdo.bbc.co.uk/hi/english/static/events/reith_2000/lecture6.stm> (March 2002).

Huntington, E. (1915) *Civilization and Climate*, New Haven: Yale University Press.

Ingold, T. (1993) 'Globes and spheres', in K. Milton (ed.) *Environmentalism: The View from Anthropology*, London: Routledge.

IPCC (1990) *Scientific Assessment of Climate change*, Report of Working Group I, J. T. Houghton, G. J. Jenkins and J. J. Ephraums (eds), Cambridge, UK: Cambridge University Press.

IPCC (1995) *Summary for policymakers: The science of climate change – IPCC Working Group I*, Intergovernmental Panel on Climate Change, Online. Available HTTP: <http://www.ipcc.ch/pub/sarsum1.htm> (February 2002).

IPCC (2001a) *Climate change 2001: The scientific basis*, Intergovernmental Panel on Climate Change, Online. Available HTTP: <http://www.grida.no/climate/ipcc_tar/wg1/index.htm> (January 2002).

IPCC (2001b) *Climate Change 2001: Synthesis Report*, Intergovernmental Panel on Climate Change, Online. Available HTTP: <http://www.grida.no/climate/ipcc_tar/syr/index.htm> (January, 2002).

ISO (1980) *ISO 6240–Performance standards in building – contents and presentation*, Geneva: International Standards Organisation.

ISO (1984a) *ISO 6241–Performance standards in building – principles for their preparation and factors to be considered*, Geneva: International Standards Organisation.

ISO (1984b) *ISO 7730–Moderate thermal environments – determination of PMV and PPD indices and specification of the conditions for thermal comfort*, Geneva: International Standards Organisation.

Jameson, F. (1994) *The Seeds of Time*, New York: Columbia University Press.

Jenks, C. (1993) *Heteropolis*, London: Academy Editions.

Johnson, P-A. (1994) *The Theory of Architecture: Concepts, Themes and Practices*, New York: Van Nostrand Reinhold.

Jones, D. L. (1998) *Architecture and the Environment*, Woodstock and New York: The Overlook Press.

Kant, I. (1996) *The Metaphysics of Morals*, trans and edited by M. Gregor, Cambridge: Cambridge University Press.

Katz, D. and Kahn, R. L. (1966) *The Social Psychology of Organisations*, New York: Wiley.

King, R. H. (2000) 'Environmental ethics and built environment', *Environmental Ethics*, 22(2): 115–31.

Koch, T. (1994) 'Establishing rigour in qualitative research: The decision trail', *Journal of Advanced Nursing* 19: 976–86.

Kortman, J., van Ewijk, H., Mak, J., Anink, D. and Knapen, M. (1998) 'Eco-quantum the LCA-based computer tool for the quantitative determination of the environmental impact of buildings', paper presented at Buildings and Environment in Asia Conference, Singapore.

Lacasse, M. A. and Vanier, D. J. (1996) 'A review of service life and durability issues', National Research Council Canada, Institute for Research in Construction. Online. Available HTTP: <http://www.nrc.ca/irc/belcam/7DBMCML_ToC.html> (March 2002).

Landscheidt, T. (2002) *El Niño Forecast Revisited*, Online. Available HTTP: <http://www.john-daly.com/sun-enso/revisit.htm> (March 2002).

Lang, J. (1987) *Creating Architectural Theory*, New York: Van Nostrand Reinhold.

Larsson, N. K. and Cole, R. J. (1998) 'A second-generation environmental performance assessment system for buildings', in *Proceedings of Green Building Challenge '98 Conference*. Online. Available HTTP: <http://www.greenbuilding.ca/gbc98cnf/speakers/larsson.htm> (November 2001).

Lea, D. (1994) 'Passport to paradise', *Perspectives*, 1(6): 40–1.

Lloyd Jones, D. (1988) *Architecture and the Environment*, Woodstock and New York: The Overlook Press.

Lloyd Wright, F. (1954) *The Natural House*, New York: Horizon Press.

Lomborg, B. (2001) *The Skeptical Environmentalist: Measuring the Real State of the World*, London: Cambridge University Press.

Lovelock, J. (1987) *Gaia. A New Look at Life on Earth*, Oxford, New York: Oxford University Press (reprinted with new preface; original publication 1979).

Lynch, K. (1960) *The Image of the City*, Cambridge, Massachusetts: Technology Press.

Lynch, K. (1976) *Managing the Sense of a Region*, Cambridge, Massachusetts: MIT Press.

Lynch, K. (1984) *Good City Form*, Cambridge, Massachusetts: MIT Press.

McDonough, William and Partners (1992) *The Hannover Principles, Design for sustainability*, Online. Available HTTP: <http://www.mcdonough.com/principles.pdf> (March, 2002).

McHarg, I. (1969) *Design with Nature*, New York: Doubleday/Natural History Press.

Macherey, P. (1966) *Towards a Theory of Literary Production*, trans. G. Wall, London, Boston: Routledge and Kegan Paul.

Markham, S. F. (1944) *Climate and the Energy of Nations*, London: Oxford University Press.

Markus, T. A. and Morris, E. N. (1980) *Buildings, Climate and Energy*, London; Marshfield, Massachusetts: Pitman.

Markus, T. A., Whyman, P., Morgan, J. D. Whitton, Maver, T., Canter, D. and Flemming, J. (1972) *Building Performance*, London: Applied Science.

Maxman, S. A. (1993) 'Shaking the rafters', *Earthwatch*, July/August: 11.

Meadows, D. (1972) *Limits to growth: a report for the Club of Rome's project on the predicament of mankind*, London: Potomac Associates.

Merriam-Webster (1994) *Collegiate Dictionary*, 10th edn, CD-Rom, Merriam-Webster Inc.

Mill, J. S. (1861) *Utilitarianism*, London: Longmans, Green & Co.

Mills, C. A. (1946) *Climate Makes the Man*, London: Victor Gollancz.

Naess, A. (1986) 'Self-realization: an ecological approach to being in the world', *The Fourth Keith Roby Memorial Lecture in Community Science*, Perth: Murdoch University.

Naess, A. (1989) *Ecology, Community and Lifestyle: An Outline of Ecosophy*, trans and revised by D. Rothenberg, Cambridge: Cambridge University Press.

NASEO (2000) *National Home Energy Rating Technical Guidelines*, National Association of State Energy Official, Online. Available HTTP: <http://www.natresnet.org/techguide/default.htm> (December 2001).

Newell, P. and Paterson, M. (1998) 'A climate for business: global warming, the state and capital', *Review of International Political Economy*, 5(4): 679–703.

Nicol, J. F. (2001) 'Characterising occupant behaviour in buildings: towards a stochastic model of occupant use of windows, lights, blinds, heaters and fans', in R. Lamberts, C. Negrao and J. Hensen (eds), *Proceedings of 7th IBPSA Building Simulation Conference BS '01 Vol 2*, Rio de Janeiro: International Building Performance Simulation Association.

Norberg-Schulz, C. (1988) *Architecture: Meaning and Place*, New York: Electa/Rizzoli.

Odum, H. T. (1970) *Environment, Power, and Society*, New York: John Wiley & Sons.

OED (1989) *Oxford English Dictionary*, Oxford: Clarendon Press.

O'Hara, S. U. (1996) 'Discursive ethics in ecosystem valuation and environmental policy', *Ecological Economics*, 16: 95–107.

O'Hara, S. U. (1998) 'Economics, ethics and sustainability: redefining connections', *International Journal of Social Economics*, 25(1): 43–62.

Olgyay, V. and Olgyay, A. (1963) *Design with Climate: Bioclimatic Approach to Architectural Regionalism*, Princeton: Princeton University Press.

Oliver, P. (2000) 'Ethics and vernacular architecture', in W. Fox (ed) *Ethics and the Built Environment*, London: Routledge.

Oliver, P. (ed.) (1972) *Shelter in Greece*, Athens: Architecture in Greece Press.

Parfit, D. (1984) *Reasons and Persons*, Oxford: Oxford University Press.

Partridge, E. (1981) 'Why Care About the Future?', in E. Partridge (ed.) *Responsibilities To Future Generations*, New York: Promethueus Books.

Paterson, M. (1996) *Global Warming and Global Politics*, London: Routledge.

Pears, A. (2001) *Pitfalls in consideration of energy in life cycle analysis*, unpublished paper, presented at seminar RMIT Centre for Design, Melbourne.

Pennington, N. and Hastie, R. (1988) 'Explanation-based decision making: effects of memory structure on judgement', *Journal of Experimental Psychology* 14(3): 521–33.

Pérez-Gómez, A. (1983) *Architecture and the Crisis of Modern Science*, Cambridge, Massachusetts: MIT Press.

Popper, K. R. (1972) *Conjectures and Refutations: The Growth of Scientific Knowledge* 4th edn, London: Routledge and Kegan Paul.

Powell, R. (1999) *Rethinking the Skyscraper: The Complete Architecture of Ken Yeang*, London: Thames and Hudson.

Pratt, V. (2000) *Environmental Philosophy*, with J. Howarth and E. Brady, London: Routledge.

Price, C. (1993) *Time, Discounting and Value*, Oxford, UK: Blackwell Publishers.

Radford, A. D. and Clark, G. (1972) 'Cyclades: studies of a building vernacular', in O. Doumanis and P. Oliver (eds), *Shelter in Greece*, Athens: Architecture in Greece Press.

Radford, A. D. and Gero, J. S. (1988) *Design by Optimization in Architecture, Building and Construction*, New York: Van Nostrand Reinhold Co.

Rawls, J. (1972) *A Theory of Justice*, Oxford: Clarendon Press.

Redclift, M. R. (1994) 'Sustainable development: economics and the environment', in M. R. Redclift and C. Sage (eds) *Strategies for Sustainable Development: Local Agendas for the Southern Hemisphere*, Chichester and New York: J. Wiley & Sons.

Rees, J. (1997) 'Tube house indoor air quality', unpublished Advanced Studies in Architecture Report, The University of Adelaide Department of Architecture.

Rees, W. E. (1999) *The Built Environment and the Ecosphere: A Global Perspective*, Online. Available HTTP: <http://www.nesea.org/buildings/images/Built%20Environ.rtf> (February 2002).

République Française (1997) *Second National Communication of France under the Climate Convention*, Online. Available HTTP: <http://unfccc.int/resource/docs/natc/france2.pdf> (March 2002).

Rittel, H. W. J. and Webber, M. M. (1973) 'Dilemmas in a general theory of planning', *Policy Sciences* 4: 155–69.

Ross, A. (1994) *The Chicago Gangster Theory of Life*, London: Verso.

Rudofsky, B. (1964) *Architecture Without Architects: A Short Introduction to Non-Pedigreed Architecture*, New York: Doubleday.

Santamouris, M., Papanikolaou, N., Livada, I., Koronakis, I., Georgakis, C., Argiriou, A. and Assimakopolous, D. N. (2001) 'On the impact of urban climate on the energy consumption of buildings', *Solar Energy*, 70(3): 201–16.

Schön, D. A. (1982) *The Reflective Practitioner*, New York: Basic Books.

Schön, D. A. (1987) *Educating the Reflective Practitioner*, San Francisco: Jossey-Bass.

Seidl, I. and Tisdell, C. A. (1999) 'Carrying capacity reconsidered: from Malthus' population theory to cultural carrying capacity', *Ecological Economics* 31: 395–408.

Smith, M., Whitelegg, J. and Williams, N. (1998) *Greening the Built Environment*, London: Earthscan Publications.

Smithdale, P. C. and Thompson, M. W. (2000) *Should new houses in the UK be of lightweight or heavyweight construction?*, Online. Available HTTP: <http://ceca.uel.ac.uk/aees/research/sibwood/shoulditbewood.html> (January, 2002).

Smithson, M. (1988) *Ignorance and Uncertainty: Emerging Paradigms*, New York: Springer Verlag.

Soebarto, V. and Williamson, T. J. (2001) 'Multi-criteria assessment of building performance: theory and implementation', *Environment and Building*, 36: 681–90.

Spector, T. (2001) *The Ethical Architect*, Princeton: Princeton Architectural Press.

Steele, J. (1997) *An Architecture for People: The Complete Works of Hassan Fathy*, London: Thames and Hudson.

Stein, J. R. (1997) *Accuracy of Home Energy Rating Systems, LBNL Report No. 40394*, California: Lawrence Berkeley National Laboratory, Online. Available HTTP: <http://eetd.lbl.gov/EA/Reports/40394/> (December 2001).

Sulle, C. (1993) 'Environment, EDF veut donner le "LA"', *Le Magazine de la Construction*, 54 (May): 7.

Sutherland Shire Council (1997) 'Environmental sustainability index' (*Draft*), Sutherland, Australia: Sutherland Shire Council.

Sylvan, R. and Bennett, D. (1994) *The Greening of Ethics*, Cambridge: White Horse Press and Tucson: The University of Arizona Press.

Teymur, N. (1982) *Environmental Discourse: A Critical Analysis of 'Environmentalism' in Architecture, Planning, Design, Ecology, Social Sciences, and the Media*, London: ?uestion Press.

Tickell, O. (1999) Reported in *The Guardian* (London), 14 April.

UIA (1993) *Declaration of interdependence for a sustainable future*, UIA/AIA World Congress of Architects, Chicago, 18–21 June 1993, Union Internationale d'Architecture, Online. Available HTTP: <http://www.uia-architectes.org/texte/summary/p2b1.html> (March 2002).

UK (1997) *Climate Change – The United Kingdom programme: The United Kingdom's Second Report under the Framework Convention on Climate Change*, Online. Available HTTP: <http://unfccc.int/resource/docs/natc/uknc2.pdf> (March 2002).

United Nations (1992a) *United Nations Framework Convention on Climate Change*, Online. Available HTTP: <http://www.unfccc.de/> (March 2002).

United Nations (1992b) *Agenda 21*, Online. Available HTTP: <http://www.igc.org/habitat/agenda21/index.html> (May 2002).

United Nations (1992c) *United Nations Convention on Biological Diversity*, Online. Available HTTP: <http://www.biodiv.org/convention/articles.asp> (May 2002).

United Nations (1992d) *United Nations Convention to Combat Desertification in Those Countries Experiencing Serious Drought and/or Desertification, Particularly in Africa*, Online. Available HTTP: <http://www.unccd.int/convention/text/convention.php> (May 2002).

United Nations (1997) *The Kyoto Protocol to the United Nations Framework Convention on Climate Change*, Online. Available HTTP: <http://www.unfccc.int/resource/docs/cop3/07aol.pdf> (May 2002).

UNFCCC (1992) *Article 2, United Nations Framework Convention on Climate Change*, Online. Available HTTP: <http://www.unfccc.de/> (March 2002).

US Energy Policy Act (1992) *Voluntary Rating Guidelines, Section 271 (b) 4*. Online: Available HTTP: <http://energy.nfesc.navy.mil/docs/law_us/92epact/hr776toc.htm> (March 2002).

US State Department (1997) *Climate Action Report: 1997 Submission of the United States of America Under the United Nations Framework Convention on Climate Change*, Online. Available HTTP: <http://unfccc.int/resource/docs/natc/usnc2.pdf> (March 2002).

Vale, R., Vale, B. and Fay, R. (2001) *NABERS* – 'National Australian Building Environmental Rating System', Report 3, Canberra: Environment Australia.

van Straaten, J. F. (1967) *Thermal Performance of Buildings*, Amsterdam: Elsevier.

Vitruvius (1960) *Vitruvius: The Ten Books on Architecture*, trans M. H. Morgan, New York: Dover Publications Inc.

von Bertalanffy, L. (1971) *General System Theory: Foundations, Development, Applications*, London: Allen Lane.

von Bonsdorff, P. (1993) 'Perceived ecology: the real and the symbolic in architecture', in T. Oksala (ed.) *Design: Ecology, Aesthetics, Ethics*, Proceedings of DEcon '93 Special Focus Symposium of INTERSYMP '93, Baden-Baden: The International Institute for Systems Research and Cybernetics.

WCED (1990) 'Our common future (The Brundtland Report)', Melbourne: World Commission on Environment and Development (First published 1987, Oxford: Oxford University Press).

Were, J. (1989) 'Air is stupid (It can't follow the arrows)', unpublished paper presented at the ANZSES Building Group Conference, Hobart.

White, A. R. (1984) *Rights*, Oxford: Clarendon Press.

White, L. Jr (1967) 'The historical roots of our ecological crisis', *Science*, 155: 1203–7.

Williamson, T. J. and Erell, E. (2001) 'Thermal Performance Simulation and the Urban Micro-Climate: Measurements and Prediction' in R. Lamberts, C. Negrão, and J. Hensen (eds), *Proceedings of IBPSA Conference BS' 01*, Rio de Janerio: International Building Performance Simulation Association.

Williamson, T. J. and Riordan, P. (1997) 'Thermostat strategies for discretionary heating and cooling of dwellings in temperate climates', in J. D. Spitler and J. L. M. Hensen (eds), *Proceedings of the 5th IBPSA Building Simulation Conference*, Vol. 1, Prague: International Building Performance Simulation Association.

Williamson, T. J., O'Shea, S. and Menadue, V. (2001) 'NatHERS: science and non-science', in W. Osterhaus and J. McIntosh (eds), *Proceedings of the 35th ANZAScA Conference*. School of Architecture, Victoria University of Wellington, NZ: Australia and New Zealand Architectural Science Association (Published on CD).

Wittmann, S. (1997) 'Architect's perceptions Regarding Barriers To Sustainable Architecture', unpublished PhD dissertation, Sydney: The University of New South Wales.

Wright, J. R. (1970) 'Measurement – key to performance', *Performance of Buildings: Concept and Measurement – Building Science series 1*, Washington: US Department of Commerce.

Wright, F. L. (1971) *The Natural House*, New York: Horizon Press.

WTO (1994) *Agreement on Technical Barriers to Trade*, Geneva: World Trade Organization, Online: Available HTTP <http://www.wto.org/english/docs_e/legal_e/17-tbt.pdf> (July 2002).

Yeang, K. (1995) *Designing with Nature: The Ecological Basis for Architectural Design*, New York: McGraw-Hill.

Yeang, K. (1996) *The Skyscraper Bioclimatically Considered*, London: Academy Editions.

Index